Is Punishment Ethical?

The Fallacy of Good and Evil

Also by ♥ Jeanine Joy

True Prevention—Optimum Health: Remember Galileo

Prevent Suicide: The Smart Way

"Trusting One's Emotional Guidance Builds Resilience", Perspectives on Coping and Resilience. Ed. Venkat Pulla, Shane Warren, and Andrew Shatté. Laxmi Nagar: Authors Press, 2013. 254-279

"Develop A Successful and Resilient Mindset", Success Uncovered, Editor: Kizzi Nkwocha: Mithra Publishing, 2015, 27-39

More Books Coming Soon by ♥ Jeanine Joy

Our Children Live in a War Zone: The Truth about Good and Evil, A Plan to Bring Peace to our Homes, Streets, and World

*Become **More** Resilient: The Smart Way, Be Ready for Life*

Diversity Appreciation: Using Science to Transform the Paradigm

Empowered Employees are Engaged Employees

18 Extra Healthy, Happy Years

BLOOM: Your Keys to Happiness

Emotional Agility: The Smarter Way

Success: The Smart Way

Thrive More, Now Publishing

Is Punishment Ethical? The Fallacy of Good and Evil
A Thrive More, Now Book / November 2015

Published by
Thrive More, Now Publishing
Charlotte, North Carolina

Thrive More Now Publishing
Rights Department
P.O. Box 6888
Concord NC 28078

For information about special discounts for bulk purchases or speaking engagements, please contact Thrive More, Now Publishing.

Keywords: social justice, criminal justice reform, good and evil, is punishment ethical, is punishment moral, emotional guidance, disparate impact, criminal justice system, restorative justice, root cause, primary prevention

ISBN-13: 978-0692490280
ISBN-10: 0692490280

Forward

It is important to understand what this book has the potential to accomplish and what it does not claim the ability to accomplish.

If the suggestions in this book are embraced and widely taught, the flow of new inmates in both juvenile and adult incarceration facilities could slow to a trickle. That would release resources that could be used to reduce crime even more. In a single decade we could stop mass incarceration. Forever.

This book provides a form of Primary Prevention designed to prevent behaviors that result in lives lived in ways that are harmful to self and others. The applications for this information are broader than criminal justice reform, but this is an area where some of the most pain suffered by individuals, families and communities can be ended. Primary Preventions are designed to prevent problems from manifesting in the first place instead of waiting for a problem to arise and dealing with it when it is bigger and more difficult to solve.

The same techniques can reduce the incidents of undesired behaviors by law enforcers because the root of bad behavior by both criminals and police officers is the same.

I do not claim that these techniques will help every individual who is incarcerated. It can help many of them and I am calling for an opportunity to provide training that is studied so that we can learn more about its ability to reduce recidivism and improve the quality of life for those who are, or have been, incarcerated.

This book represents over twenty years of research focused on one question, "What makes humans thrive?" More than a decade was spent pursuing the answer and almost seven years have been devoted to finding practical ways to apply the answer in ordinary lives in ways that individuals with any worldview (religious, spiritual, or scientific) find palatable.

Just like with a tree or any living thing, when the root or core is healthy, the systems comprising the living system flourish. The root of the answer to human thriving is mindset or beliefs. Because this solution begins at the root, it affects the entire being: physical, mental, emotional and behavioral health as well as relationships, and success in everything that is important to individuals.

Changes that begin from the inside and expand outward are far easier to implement and sustain than changes that attempt to work from the outside and move inward.

The benefits of implementing the solution offered in this thesis extend far beyond greatly reducing crime even though that is far more than any symptom based solution can ever hope to accomplish.

We must think longer term than mere reaction to symptoms if we are to solve this problem.

If we focus only on those who are already in the system, the flood of new individuals entering the system will continue to swell. By stopping the flood, we will have greater resources with which to help those who are in the system. If we do not stop the flood of new arrivals, there will never be enough resources to stop this chain of pain.

Jeanine Joy

Acknowledgements

I have far more than most to appreciate. First, I want to acknowledge my husband, Phil, for his willingness to support the time and effort I've devoted to acquiring this knowledge and pursuing credentials that demonstrate the level of my knowledge and of course, my appreciation of his unconditional love and of the love I feel for him.

The concepts presented in this book are the culmination of every book I've read, every encounter I've had, and my unique perception thereof.

I must acknowledge those whose behavior toward me was less than desired for building my desire to understand the connection between behavior and emotional state. I gained valuable insights from each of them, for which I am grateful. I've gained just as many insights, of a different sort, from the daughters I've been blessed with—not because their behavior has been bad—but because they are so different from one another and from me. They helped me understand the uniqueness of all, which helped me become a person who deeply appreciates differences and sees the value of them.

I am truly blessed by a life that is perfect…and that keeps getting better.

Introduction

Two things are clear throughout recorded history. The first is that societies have been concerned with and attempted to control the behavior of citizens. The second is that they have not had much success controlling behavior. Ever-increasing punishments, rules, and enforcement efforts demonstrate that this battle is not being won.

One aspect of behavior that is evident as soon as it is consciously considered is seldom consciously recognized by society because our current paradigm does not take it into consideration. That is the fact that happy people are not behaving in ways society finds undesirable. Think about every criminal you are aware of, from terrorists and mass murderers to white collar criminals. They're not happy and the more heinous the crime, the longer they have been unhappy.

To make the point intended by this thesis three concepts require clarification, five commonly believed concepts are refuted, and a new concept is introduced. All must be understood at deep levels in order for the premise of this book to be fully understood. The difference between a transitory state of happiness and True Happiness is defined. Clarifying information about emotions and perspective and its relationship to individuals is provided. The concept that emotions are feedback from a sensory feedback system is introduced and the supporting science is explained.

Documentation from a wide variety of sources support my premises. Research that demonstrates that humans are kinder,[1] less racist,[2] more inclusive,[3] less likely to commit crimes,[4] and have better relationships with others when they feel good and that these things worsen as emotional stance declines. Although the health and cognitive benefits of positive emotions are tremendous, I point to those primarily as evidence that we are designed to feel good. I describe the basics of Emotional Guidance and its use to achieve and maintain a state of thriving.

Realizing that many people who read this book may assume that I, or someone close to me, has been incarcerated—I feel the need to point out this would be an inaccurate assumption. In fact, there have been numerous times in my life when I have experienced things that the perpetrators of are commonly punished for. My position on this issue is not one I was taught or believed at early ages. It developed from my understanding of how emotions affect behavior and then realizing that the usual response to bad behavior exacerbates the problem rather than reducing or ending it. I am an advocate for this because I believe it will solve a major social problem that creates a lot of unnecessary suffering in our world and because when the facts are understood and the techniques have been practiced, it makes perfect sense. You hold in your hands hope for a better world.

Once the relationship between emotional state and behavior is clear, it also becomes clear that punishment worsens future behavior.

I have been aided in my understanding by a long-term desire to understand what makes humans thrive—a question I have been asking for over twenty years. It is a big question, but I've learned that we get the answers we seek.

I've studied this issue from three perspectives, scientific, religious, and spiritual. Some of the explanations are based on a belief in a higher power, what many would call God. However, I also include a scientific basis that someone who does not believe in God can focus on to understand and apply the concepts presented in their own life. I think it is easier to achieve a positive mindset with the support of a belief in God, but I recognize that about 14% of the world's population does not believe and I want to help everyone, not just those who have religious or spiritual beliefs that include God.

My intent is to present one concept that everyone can benefit from understanding. When I first began teaching I learned that many people with a religious worldview wanted to see how what I was teaching fit into their worldview. I studied six major world religions to determine if the key tenets of what I was teaching were consistent with the texts of their religion. The answer was always yes. The tenets aren't the focus of the religion, but they were there in the words of their holy books.

I conclude by suggesting implementation of a global program that teaches individuals how to understand their Emotional Guidance combined with a complete shift in the way we respond to undesired behaviors beginning at young ages. It is not a shift to permissiveness that allows wild behavior, but to one that comprehends at a deep level, that anyone exhibiting undesired behavior is emotionally feeling less than their best and that the most effective way to ensure the behavior does not continue is to gently guide the person to better feeling emotional states. Both the 2-year old having a tantrum and the mass murderer are expressing that they have emotions that feel less good than they want to feel. By teaching children how to manage stress and their emotional state to healthy levels, we can greatly decrease the likelihood that the child will behave in abhorrent ways in the future.

It's far easier to prevent someone from becoming a criminal than to heal them after they have developed unhealthy habits of thought. It can be done, but by stopping the flood of youthful offenders that keep the prisons full, more resources will be available to help those who are already part of the school to prison pipeline.

Table of Contents

Contents

Important Notice

Do not read this book. Reading it will provide only an intellectual understanding.

You must apply the ideas presented to your own life to truly understand its power to change your emotional state. You must actually feel the shift in your own emotional state as the result of deliberate application of these techniques to grasp the difference even small shifts can make in your outlook and the way it changes your thought processes.

It takes time to begin to grasp the magnitude of the potential using this information has. In many ways, it is like learning to walk. You begin with baby steps and soon you're off and running. You must be patient with yourself. You must love yourself. If you don't, the techniques in this book will aid with that as well.

For most people, nothing they've ever done (or will do) will have as much positive impact on their lives as learning to use and applying these techniques in their own life.

Emotional Guidance

"...man must evolve for all human conflict a method which rejects revenge, aggression and retaliation. The foundation of such a method is love."

This thesis lays out a methodology to accomplish the goal Dr. Martin Luther King Jr. so eloquently spoke of in his acceptance speech for the Nobel Peace Prize in 1964.[5]

A brief introduction to the concept of Emotional Guidance is required before we delve into the other aspects of this book; additional details will be covered later. In James Allen's *As a Man Thinketh*, he wrote, "Such is the conscious master, and man can only thus become by discovering within himself the laws of thought; which discovery is totally a matter of application, self-analysis, and experience."[6] Although I believe Mr. Allen was referencing meditation, the same could be said of Emotional Guidance—understanding of it is totally a matter of application, self-analysis, and experience.

Emotions are a response to our thoughts. Since I am privy only to my own thoughts and emotions, I can only guess at the thoughts another has thought that led to the emotional state he or she is experiencing. Because emotional states can have both inner and outer signs, we sometimes believe we understand how another feels. When we do, our minds immediately create a *back story* for why the person feels as they do. While that *back story* will consider things we know about the other person, the *back story* is largely built upon what would make us feel thus and often has little to do with why the other person feels the way they feel.[7]

If we cannot easily find a *back story* that makes the others' emotional state seem rational or justified, we may find fault with their emotional state—as if their current emotional state was somehow wrong. The parent who tells the child to "Shut-up and stop crying or you'll be given something to cry about," is demonstrating this quite clearly—albeit, with poor parenting skills. Obviously, from the child's perspective, she already has something to cry about.

For every thought we think, there is an emotional response. That emotional response is actually intended to guide us toward self-realization and away from danger. The correct interpretation is simple. If the emotional response to a thought feels better than the prior thought (an improvement in the emotion), the new thought is moving closer to self-realization. If the thought elicits the same emotion as the prior thought, no motion forward or backward was made by the thought. If the emotion feels worse, then the new thought is moving further from self-realization, possibly toward danger, and certainly toward a less desirable outcome.

Today most people misinterpret their emotional responses, often believing that negative emotion validates the truth of the thought. When I first began consciously understanding my guidance, I looked back at my life and could see clearly that I was guided to things that led to the fulfillment of my highest good—even when the path seemed to make a wrong turn, I could see the rightness of it from the larger perspective.

Happiness Defined

Society is littered with false premises about what causes happiness and even what happiness is. Commercials increasingly tell consumers that a product will make them happy. Most people believe it is their mate's (or children's) responsibility to make them happy. Fleeting positive emotions are not happiness and do not provide the benefits to individuals or society that True Happiness brings. Products do not cause happiness and mates and children cannot make someone happy. We can perceive them in ways that feel good, but the way we perceive others is our choice.

True Happiness is created in the mind of the individual feeling happiness and is a result of the perspective the individual is taking about the subject they are focused upon. For example, Coca-Cola advertises that their product causes happiness with their slogan, *Open Happiness*. A man who wants a Coke™ may feel transitory happiness when he opens a Coke™ but a man who wanted a beer may feel less than happy when he is given a Coke™ instead of a beer. Individual perspective is the deciding factor that determines the degree of happiness, not the product or situation.

Anyone who has attempted to make someone happy when that person was determined to be angry knows that they cannot make someone feel better unless and until the person decides they no longer want to be angry. No one has the power to make someone else happy. Each person has the ability to choose perspectives about any situation that feel good or bad. Every particle in the Universe contains both aspects.[8] Each of us has the ability to choose which aspects we focus on at any given moment. That choice results in our degree of happiness or unhappiness.

I define True Happiness as:

"The state of True Happiness does not require a constant state of bliss. It is a deep sense of inner stability, peace, well-being, and vitality that is consistent and sustainable. Awareness that one possesses the knowledge and skills to return to a happy state, even when not in that state, is a critical component of sustainable happiness. True Happiness is sustainable because the individual deliberately and consciously chooses perspectives that create positive emotions and has cultivated this habit of thought until his or her natural and habitual response focuses on the positive aspects of any situation."

True Happiness is the result of both a habit of thought and a set of skills that empowers the individual to know, with great faith, that there are positive aspects of every situation.

In this book, happiness refers to this definition of true and sustainable happiness.

While True Happiness may seem to be a pie-in-the-sky Pollyannaish viewpoint, because it is skill-based, any sufficiently motivated individual can develop the habits of thought and apply simple skills to achieve it and enjoy the many benefits that are the natural outcome of sustaining a positive outlook.

The basis of happiness (what makes a person happy) varies from person to person. There are some common themes such as having a larger purpose, but the basis of any individual's happiness is as unique as their fingerprints because our goals are unique and it is positive motion toward our goal(s) that creates positive emotion, even if that positive motion is only a shift toward a more empowered mindset.

Fleeting positive emotions felt when someone achieves a desired goal pale in comparison to True Happiness. One is like a Mayfly and the other as reliable as the Earth.

Relativity

How any given situation makes us feel is relative; no two people respond in exactly the same way—even to the exact same situation. Many people remember their very first home away from their parents' home. Even a one-bedroom or studio apartment is often a source of great pride and happiness during the early stages of independence. The same apartment a decade later might be the cause of significant unhappiness. The expectation of where one will live during a particular stage of life has a more significant effect on the degree of satisfaction experienced than the actual circumstances. At 18, my first apartment was in a rundown area of downtown Sacramento with a small, dark galley kitchen and no dishwasher. I was excited and proud of my financial independence even when it was impossible to sleep on hot nights without air conditioning. A couple of years later, when I purchased my first home, that apartment would have been viewed much differently.

Humans tend to project how we would feel in any given situation onto others who are experiencing the situation. We often experience more angst thinking about undesirable circumstances than those who are actually living those circumstances feel because of the relativity of the circumstances to their expectations and desires. We even project our very human perceptions onto our animals, ignoring the fact that our animals tend to focus in a much more general way that then helps them maintain more positive emotions.

If you doubt that animals tend to focus on the positive, lock your dog in the trunk of your car for a minute during mild weather. See how happy he is when you open the trunk. Imagine the reaction you would receive if you locked your spouse in the trunk for the same length of time—it would not be the joyous greeting your dog gave you. Your human spouse would see the situation with much greater detail, blaming you for locking him or her in the trunk instead of focusing on the positive aspect—that you released them from the dark and confining space.

Yet your spouse could focus more generally and feel happy to see you. Most would not focus that way—but it is possible to do so. A spouse who cares most about feeling good and who has practiced skills that create sustainable happiness could respond more like your dog.[a] With the right mindset, it would be possible for your spouse to trust you enough to nap, meditate, or vi sualize while in the trunk, thereby suffering even less

---

[a] I am not suggesting tolerating inappropriate behavior, this is an exaggerated example used only to make the point.

emotional angst than the dog. Each of us has the ability to weild that much power over our own emotional state, but we will only achieve it if we practice.

Why would we want to have power over our emotional state? We are motivated by what we believe will feel best to us. When we leave our happiness up to the wims of others we cannot reach our potential for joy. We are at our best when we are happy, so when we don't have control of our emotional state we have less control over our destiny.

When we have control over our emotional state we can enjoy situations that are not considered enjoyable. I do this at the dentist. Several years ago I had some extensive dental work done that required me to be in the chair with my mouth open for several hours. I spent the time visualizing and actually had a good time. Afterwards, my dentist began apologizing for how long it took and I responded, "Are you kidding? Do you know how seldom I get that much time in my happy place?" By practicing going to my happy place in advance, I was able to enjoy being in my happy (mental) place even under uncomfortable circumstances, which means I did not experience any discomfort.

Even when someone else suffers an unthinkable tragedy such as the loss of a child, it is common for those hearing of the circumstances to feel worse than the person who has suffered the loss (while they imagine how they believe they would feel under those circumstances). Imagine that the child who died had been in and out of trouble so often the parent expected to receive that call someday while your child is well-behaved, so you seldom think about something undesired happening.

A friend of mine who recently lost her son to suicide described this in the week after his death, "I had no idea how much weight I was carrying around, and waiting for this phone call during all the years we tried to help him. It's only now that the call has come that I realize how much anticipating and fearing the call weighed on me every day." (private conversation)[9] The difference between what you feel when you imagine how you'd feel if it were your child and your current reality is far greater than the difference between what the other parent expected and her reality. It does not mean it is not a bad situation, but playing the mind game of "How would I feel?" is a pointless exercise because we cannot accurately judge the relativity of another person's experiences. Relativity has a direct bearing on the degree of negative emotion felt in any given situation.

My friend was mourning her loss and sad, but she also realized the weight she had been carrying as she waited more than a decade for the phone call that would tell her that her troubled son was gone. She had done all she could, but had not been able to reach him and she knew this, which led to her living in a constant state of tension, anticipating that she could receive bad news at any time. It was only after the worst had happened, and the weight lifted from her that she realized how much stress she had been living with.

Someone whose child is thriving might feel worse in their imagining the loss of their child than my friend does in the actual loss of her child. It is not that she loved him less, but that her expectations about her son's future were not as high. The difference between her expectation and her reality was not that far apart, whereas someone whose child is thriving has expectations that are vastly different.

Unless we are very conscious about not doing so, we tend to think others should perceive as we do—but it is not really possible. For example, when I took my daughters for college visits, the way I thought they would think about the dorm rooms—in fact, the way **I thought they should think**—was very different from how they thought about them. If my parents had been willing to send me to college and pay for housing while I had the freedom of living away from home and the education I wanted, any sort of dorm room would have made me ecstatic. My children were accustomed to much nicer accommodations than I had as a child including their own bathroom and fewer parental mandates about their behavior. Their desire for freedom was far lower than mine was at their age, so it did not offset the perceived lowering of the standard of living from what they were accustomed to that necessitated by living in a dormitory.

I perceived the dorm rooms in the way I thought I would have viewed them as a teenager and projected that perception onto how I thought my daughters should perceive them. At first I attempted to argue and bring them around to my viewpoint, but it quickly became apparent that I had to accept that they had a different perspective than I would have had at their age. I was able to appreciate that the reasons their perspectives were different were positive.

We have far more control over how we perceive any given situation than most realize. We could feel fearful about a situation which would result in a pessimistic outlook and a more disempowered perspective than other possible perspectives. If we felt angry about the same situation, we would feel more optimistic and empowered.[10] Our perspective about any given situation is usually based upon habits of thought rather than thoughtful consideration of the current situation[11]

It is best to use one's own life experiences to understand Emotional Guidance. Looking at someone else's experiences does not produce the same results because our desires are unique. For example, someone whose highest priority is to remain married to their original spouse may find it difficult to believe that someone was guided to a marriage that did not last forever. This is because the person being observed had different desires. Perhaps she wanted a secure home life while she grew in other areas, and the quickest path to that was through marriage. I'm not indicating she consciously knew when she entered the marriage that it would not be her forever relationship—only that her guidance encouraged the marriage because it fulfilled her other desires. If she did not have a goal of a forever marriage, her guidance would not assert that goal into the mix.

The lack of a forever marriage goal is not (consciously) the same as a goal of not having a forever marriage.

The point is that we cannot know another's deepest wishes and dreams so what their guidance encourages them to do has no relationship to what our guidance would lead us to do.

Empathy

Empathy is the ability to understand and share the feelings of another. It is my opinion, because of the relationship of how we feel to whom we are and what our goals are, that it is not possible to feel empathy. It is also my opinion that attempting to empathize with someone who is in a low emotional state does not serve either person. In order to think like the person who is hurting is thinking, it is necessary to join them in their low emotional state. That is the only place where you would have access to thoughts similar to theirs.

As we will see later in this book, a lower mood lessens cognitive ability. When you empathize, you have no more access to solutions than the person with the problem has access to. You are of no benefit to them in any real sense of the word.

In researching several dictionaries for a clear definition of compassion, there seems to be little agreement. Definitions ranged from "a feeling of deep sympathy and sorrow for another who is stricken by misfortune, accompanied by a strong desire to alleviate the suffering" to "If a man shows kindness, caring, and a willingness to help others, he's showing compassion." Merriam-Webster's and other sources were more in line with the first definition, which is the less beneficial of the two. The first definition is essentially empathy plus a desire to help and has the same flaws as empathy. The ability to help is thwarted by joining the individual in their low emotional state.

The second definition of compassion does not require the person to join the suffering individual in his or her suffering. With that type of compassion, someone is able to help. It is possible to remain in a good emotional state, where cognitive abilities and intuition are at their best while recognizing that someone needs help. From that emotional state, another person can be of great benefit.

I am not encouraging a lack of compassion. I am encouraging individuals not to deliberately cultivate negative emotional states within themselves. Empathy does not serve a purpose and actually harms the individual, depriving him or her of moments during which she could be happy and receive and share the benefits of happiness.

I am not saying to be happy at another's misfortune or that the misfortune is theirs and not yours. The best stance you can develop for someone who is suffering is to see them in your mind's eye as they can be after they've overcome the problem—whether it is finding health and vitality following an illness, or true love after heartbreak.

Selfishness

Selfishness is another concept society has backward. When we selfishly take care of our own needs first, a natural desire to help others surfaces. But unlike those who do for others out of a sense of obligation—something that often leads to resentment—a synergy exists when a person who is already happy helps another. The helper is paid immediately in the form of good feeling emotions that come from knowing you've been of benefit. Resentment builds only when we sacrifice our own basic needs for those of another.

Sonja Lyubomirsky , the author of *The How of Happiness*, said "Compassion fosters happiness, but being sacrificial reduces wellbeing."[12] Many people have been taught to sacrifice their own happiness to serve others, but that is a flawed premise. Over time your own unhappiness robs you of the ability to offer anywhere near your potential contributions.

When our needs are satisfied, helping another, even a stranger, can be fun and joyful. We become more of our potential. It is not circumstances that determine behavior. It is a sense of satisfaction with our life and emotional state that is then reflected in pro-social behaviors.

There are two paths to kindness:
1. Managing our own emotional stance at good-feeling levels, or
2. Decide who you are (i.e. a kind person) and practice the belief of who you are until it dominates your mind. A Meditation Program can be used to develop beliefs about your own kindness and so can visualizations.

When a sustained positive emotional state is achieved, one of the first things almost everyone does is exhibit a desire for others to also enjoy that level of emotional stability. When you are truly happy—it feels better if others are too.

Perspective

The assumption that others see life as we see it is merely an assumption—one that is easily refuted by closer examination. In fact, most disagreements among humans are because the participants see the situation from different perspectives. Most people believe one perspective is right and others perspectives are wrong, but just as *good* and *evil* are false premises; the belief that only one perspective is right and all others are wrong is a false premise.

As we expand outward, looking at the perspective of two individuals who have greater differences (in experiences, beliefs, or thought processes), the variances become even more pronounced. Take a woman who is well read and compare her perspectives about specific topics to those of someone who is illiterate; the variances will be very pronounced. Take a man who has never left his hometown and compare his perspectives to those of a man who has traveled the world; the variances will be very pronounced.

There is no inherent rightness in any given perspective because it is just that, a perspective. It is an opinion formed based on the way one individual perceives the topic. From that individual's perspective, the perspective is accurate and *right*. However, someone viewing the situation from another vantage point will have a different perspective on the situation, one that is also *right* based on the vantage point he has.

Two people can have opinions that are polar opposite, yet both are right from their personal perspective. Deeper communication that looks at the underlying perspective can resolve most differences amicably. At least, if not resolved to the level of agreement, an understanding of the others' point of view can be achieved. Agreement is more likely as well—at least agreement that they could see how someone would perceive in that way. When we attempt to change someone's opinion without addressing perspective, we meet a brick wall. The tendency is to defend our conclusion, which makes us more attached to our stance.

For example, I had a client whose child was very stubborn. She viewed stubbornness as a positive trait. She credited it with giving her an advantage when she faced adversity in her life. Her husband, on the other hand, believed children should not be stubborn and actually commented more than once that they should *beat it out of her*. Clearly they had very different ideas about a strong personality trait in their child. They were not going to solve the problem at that level.

As I learned more about why they felt as they did, the Father was concerned because he felt that someone who was stubborn would resist parental dictates and that this would worsen as she progressed into the teenage years. Ultimately, his concern was for the welfare of his daughter. The Mother felt that stubbornness would help the child achieve goals even when obstacles stood in her way and could even help her keep going when others might quit. From a broader perspective, she thought stubbornness would improve her daughter's welfare.

At this level, it becomes clear that both parents are most concerned with their daughter's welfare, a strong point of agreement. They simply disagree about how to go about maximizing her welfare. But moving the conversation to this point of agreement allowed them to discuss it more rationally. They felt better, which translates directly to improved cognitive ability. Research has shown that our ability to think clearly shifts with our emotional state. The title of recent research by Maier, Makwana and Hare is *Acute Stress Impairs Self-Control in Goal-Directed Choice by Altering Multiple Functional Connections within the Brain's Decision Circuits.*[13] Stress, and particularly chronic stress, is not our friend.

When they were arguing about how to achieve their joint goal it was easy to conclude that the other parent did not care about their child's welfare because they believed that they would reach the same conclusion if they really cared. By finding the point of agreement first, they could then explore the reason they felt so strongly about how to manage her stubbornness without the emotional drama. As they dug deeper, the Father relayed that he had several experiences in his teens when he could have easily died—situations where he was stubbornly acting contrary to what his parents had demanded he act. He worried that his daughter's stubbornness would cause her to repeat his mistakes.

It is easy to see how, based on his life experiences, he would feel a stubborn child was at enough risk that breaking her stubbornness seemed like a good goal. The Mother's perspective also came from her own childhood experiences, which included abuse and failed attempts to leave the abusive environment that led to her being suicidal on several occasions. She credited her stubbornness with giving her the fortitude to continue with an attitude that she was not going to allow them to beat her. Her opinion was that her stubbornness had saved her life.

It's easy to see why their daughter's stubbornness was an emotion-filled topic. The Father perceived its presence as life-threatening and the Mother perceived it as life-saving. Once we explored why the parents felt as they did, we began talking about the child. I learned that even as a pre-teen she would immediately end friendships when her friends began behaving in ways she found unacceptable. She had high standards of behavior for herself and her friends. When she ended a friendship because the friend began drinking her parent's alcohol, her stubbornness came into play. She did not question her decision once she made it. She had defined herself as someone who followed the rules and whose friends also did.

There were more examples of when she stubbornly stuck to her personal moral code even when peer pressure was strong. It was clear her values were ones the parents approved of. It quickly became apparent that for this particular child, stubbornness was serving her and that her personal moral code was such that she would not repeat her father's youthful mistakes.

Both parents agreed that her stubbornness was serving her and that they probably did not have to worry about this child very much at all. Her stubbornness stopped being an area of discord in their marriage and actually strengthened their faith that their family would survive the teen years intact. But even more importantly, they learned to go deeper when they had a disagreement because their goal was the same, they just had different perceptions about how to achieve their goal.

Both parent's perspectives were right from the experiences from which they were looking at the situation. Only by exploring various perspectives and then comparing those to the actual situation were they able to find common ground. Everyone sees reality through filters that affect how they view every situation. The conclusions on the surface are not where problems can be easily solved. Going deeper makes solutions much easier to identify.

Humility

We are all far more powerful than most believe we are, and most are ignorant of how to wield that power. The keys are in all the holy books I've ever seen and in the writings of great minds throughout the ages—but most humans continue to ignore them. We are taught to be humble though it serves us not.

Humility is sometimes confused with not being egotistical and the two are not the same thing at all. Humility is often a type of powerlessness that indicates someone else, or a higher power, must do for you that which you believe you cannot do for yourself. Egotistical is about putting oneself above others. The best stance is one where the individual knows he or she is magnificent, a powerful and perfect creation of Source (God), sharing the planet with others who are also powerful and perfect creations of Source. "I am wonderful, and so are you," is a stance that serves us well. It is not egotistical because it does not put you above any other, but neither is it humble because it recognizes that we are a Being, created by God and part of God, with great power to create that which we desire.

It may seem I've strayed from the topic at hand, but these points are important. When one understands his or her own power s/he sees no need and has no desire to harm another to achieve his or her desires. From that empowered vantage point, it is not only unnecessary but also counterproductive to harm others. When we humbly believe we are not powerful, our potential to feel lower emotional states increases and the likelihood that we will resort to crime increases right along with it.

For example, when the economy worsens white collar crime increases. Individuals, who acted honestly in their roles, sometimes for years, can decide to steal from the employer. When the economy was strong, they felt secure and even if they were living paycheck-to-paycheck, their level of fear was not high enough to allow them to justify theft from their employer in order to improve their financial situation. But when the economy becomes shaky and they watch the news or read the newspaper detailing others who have lost their jobs and then their homes, they become fearful. In that fearful state, their cognitive abilities decrease. It becomes more difficult to reassure themselves that things will work out because from their fearful state it is literally much more difficult to think of ideas of how they would respond if they should lose their job.

Even people who are at no risk of losing their jobs, or whose skills and talents make them very marketable in a bad economy, change their behaviors during a down economy if they allow themselves to become fearful. This has a negative impact on their lives and as large numbers of people buy into the fear, it intensifies the economic downturn. It becomes a self-fulfilling prophecy. As individuals and families whose situations have not changed stop spending money on discretionary purchases like dining at restaurants, vacations, the theater, and delaying purchases of big ticket items, the economic downturn worsens.

The same fearful thinking is at work when someone steals because a family member is ill and they have high medical bills or need money for an experimental treatment. Someone taught to be humble, to not think of themselves as capable and competent, is at much greater risk of becoming fearful than someone who believes they are strong and resourceful.

It is only from the vantage point of competition, winners, losers, and *good* and *evil* that harming another finds fertile ground in the minds of men. Harm of another comes only from a lack mindset (perspective) that believes it is the only way. An empowered individual will not see any advantage in harming another person—financially, emotionally, spiritually, or physically. Belief in and trust in a loving God allows individuals to feel hopeful even when their intellect cannot find a path to what they desire. Lack of belief in a loving God can lead an individual to believe the only paths available to them are the ones they can see with cognitive abilities that are constricted as the result of a lower emotional state.

Non-Religious and Non-Spiritual View

Even if someone does not believe in a loving God, they can maintain a confident mindset that will protect them from fearful thinking. All it really takes is nurturing beliefs that make one feel empowered.

Higher Self or Ideal Self

We all have a *Higher Self* or an *Ideal Self.* Our *Higher Self* is the *True Self,* or *Whole Self* that is focusing through our physical body—the eternal self. Our *Higher Self* has always been and will always be, but our *Higher Self* is not stagnating and complete. Our *Higher Self* knows all that has been and All That Is, but is always evolving and becoming more. We create this self as we live and make decisions about whom we want to be. If we are mean to someone, we create a *Higher Self* that is nicer.[14]

We have a circular relationship with our *Higher Self.* If someone is mean to us, then we create a *Higher Self* to whom others are nicer. This *Higher* or *Ideal Self* calls us toward becoming what we've created. The *Higher Self* has vibrationally achieved all the dreams we have dreamed. Our job is to move in the direction of the *Higher Self* we have created through the living of our life. The *Higher Self* is ever-evolving as we experience life. Our desires expand our *Higher Self,* and our expanded *Higher Self* calls us to the new version of our highest level of self-realization. The *Higher Self* is unique to each of us. Although there are many common desires, no two of us want the exact same things.

Non-Religious and Non-Spiritual View

For the scientifically inclined, our *Higher Self* can be considered a thought form. To understand what a thought form is, imagine that you decide you are going to make a table. The first thought is only a thought-vibration. It may be as simple as you need a table for some purpose and the best way to get the table is to make it yourself. Once you decide to make the table, your mind begins planning how you will construct the table. You may be very deliberate about this process or you may simply see what comes to you. Decisions will be made about the size of the table and the types of materials you'll use. Now, imagine that half-way through planning your new table in your mind you are called away and don't think about the table again for several days. When you return to the idea of building the table you do not begin again with the first thought you had, the accumulation of ideas that you've had is now part of the idea of that table—as a thought-form.

You can't see this thought ft-orm, but the thoughts are definitely more than they were initially and they are together. When you begin thinking about one aspect of the table, the other thoughts return. That we cannot see thoughts or measure them does not negate that the thought about the table is more complex than the initial thought to build a table. There are ways to explain thought forms in quantum physics, but they are too complex for the purposes of this book. This is a good time to remind you that it wasn't that long ago that germs and viruses were not perceivable by human measurements. We first knew they existed by their effect on the body. We can't see gravity, but we do not doubt its existence.

We can't see radio waves, we only know they exist because we have a device (radios) that can interpret the waves and make them audible to human ears.

The *Higher Self* is a much thought about better version of us.

The religious might call the *Higher Self* our soul or spirit.

That we cannot yet measure thought-vibrations or thought-forms does not mean they do not exist. We can feel the impact of thought-vibrations and thought-forms on our emotions and we can be consciously aware of thought-forms as they expand.

There are many examples when individuals knew something existed before humanity had the capability of measuring it or even of perceiving it with something that everyone can agree upon. It has not been that long ago that a leading thinker (Ignaz Semmelweis) was ridiculed for proposing that things that were too small for us to see could cause illness and death and suggesting tht we should wash our hands to prevent their spread. During my lifetime, homeopathy was considered a hoax because no particles of the original medicine remained in the solution, at least not any that we could measure. Now new research has revealed that nanoparticles do remain. In *True Prevention — Optimum Health: Remember Galileo*, I termed the human resistance to accepting that someone thing exists when we don't have all the information but we do have enough to convince a reasonable person with an open mind that something is there, The Galileo Effect.

I'd like to think my generation is smart enough to overcome The Galileo Effect.

Uniqueness

Differences in individual desires are another area where greater understanding would serve us all well. Understanding that we each have unique desires and perspectives and that this is a wonderful thing would help us develop and sustain better personal relationships and national relationships. We can desire what we desire (we actually can't help but desire what we desire) because our lives have shown us that is what we believe is best for us. However, when we look to others for validation of our desires and dreams, we are asking if their desires and/or dreams are satisfied by our perspectives. Their perspectives really have nothing to do with our perspectives.

Our desires are valid. Our positive emotion confirms that what we desire is on our path to self-realization. One way in which people are the same is that the better a person feels emotionally, the better their behavior becomes.

For example, there are many careers I have no desire to pursue that many others feel a strong desire to do. My own career frequently has me doing something that most people fear, speaking from the stage. I love being on stage because I know it is an opportunity to help a lot of people. Many relationships, especially multi-generational ones, experience far more stress than they would if the elders understood that the next generations' dreams and desires are a powerful internal force that can not be stopped by their attempts to impose their thwarted desires onto their offspring. When I did the research for *Prevent Suicide: The Smart Way,* I read far too many stories about obedient children who pursued careers they were pressured into by their parents. Several had gone all the way through law school or medical school when they knew their heart was not in the game. It was not what they wanted to do, but it was what they had to do to please a demanding parent whose desire they put above their own.

We can use our minds to make something more compatible with our purpose than it is on the surface, but life is easier when we follow our personal goals and dreams. Children are not responsible for soothing the hurts of parent's unfulfilled dreams. Attempting to make them do so actually continues the hurt of unfulfilled dreams into another generation by distracting or preventing the child from pursuing his or her personal desires.

In *Diversity Appreciation, Using Science to Transform the Paradigm,* I elaborate more on the subject of individual differences and the value they add to the whole. When we use our Emotional Guidance, we can see clearly how individuals are encouraged by their emotions to pursue their personal goals and how they experience negative emotions when they don't.

The Emotional Guidance Solution

Emotions are literally guidance from one of our senses. The concept of *five senses* is a fallacy. New research, courtesy of the brilliant mind of Katherine Peil, and ten pages of cross-disciplinary scientific citations in her paper, *Emotion: A Self-regulatory Sense*,[15] demonstrates clearly that our emotions are a sense.[16] In fact, her position is that emotion is our oldest sense, and she uses molecular biology and the biophysical processes of living systems to lead us on a step-by-step exploration of this idea.

In her work and our discussions, Peil has explained that our emotions are output from a hitherto unrecognized sense. The function of the basic *negative* emotions is to provide information that helps us keep our bodies safe. The function of the positive emotions is to point us toward self-development and well-being. The difference between the simple organisms and most humans is that simple organisms actually listen to and respond to the emotional feedback.

Humans, on the other hand, have a tendency to ignore emotions, to suppress them, and to suffer the negative consequences of doing so in lives that are not as robust as they could be. We derive no benefits from ignoring the output from our emotional system.[17] It provides information that will improve our lives if we act upon it appropriately.

Humans tend to override the feedback from their emotional sense with **rational** thought. Yet, filters (biases) in our minds distort our perception of life. Our emotional feedback by-passes the filters and provides feedback that contains greater clarity and accuracy. This is not the only sensory feedback that humans misinterpret. Researchers have demonstrated that some people routinely misinterpret thirst as hunger and overeat because they are thirsty.[18] Psychologists call these filters biases, but I use the term filters in my work because I believe it more accurately describes the function and does not have the negative connotation that bias tends to elicit.

Our emotions do not lead us astray—although this is a common belief. Most individuals do not understand how to interpret their emotions. Emotions are not difficult to interpret accurately once one understands the language of emotions and the best way to gain greater understanding is to practice feeling emotional responses and being aware of how the emotion changes in response to changing thoughts.

Emotions are information about the gap between who we are as we think the thought that elicited the emotion and our ever expanding *Higher Self*. If we're keeping up with who our *Higher Self* is becoming we are joyful. If the gap is widening we feel worse. If the gap is continually increasing and we aren't moving forward, we're depressed or experience other low emotional states.

I am not suggesting that the solution to crime is to find a way to make everyone believe in God. That stance has led to more wars than I can count. There is another way to accomplish the same thing—one that each individual can prove to him or herself quickly and easily.

Using Emotional Guidance does not require a belief in God for two reasons. The first is that each individual has everything they need to prove the continuous presence of Emotional Guidance in their life to themselves. The second is that Emotional Guidance is supported by science. While I know Source is a loving entity that is intimately involved in every life, the ability to communicate the guidance Source provides on a scientific platform is of great value. It enables me to teach individuals with widely varying belief systems about Emotional Guidance and how to use it to increase thriving in their own life. The guidance always works, whether or not an individual believes it exists. The reason so many flounder today is not because they are not receiving Emotional Guidance—they are. But, they have been taught to misinterpret its messages and to give it less credence than their biased intellectual ability.

While individuals who develop their connection with Source on a deeper level can open communication channels that are clear, that is not necessary to receive God's gift of guidance. On the spiritual side, this quote from Abraham expands on the scientific explanation of emotional guidance.

"The Universe does not know if the vibration you are offering is because of what you are imagining, or because of what you are observing. In either case, it is responding. Where emotion comes in is that emotion is your guidance or your response to your vibration. Your emotion does not create. Emotion is your indicator of what you are already creating. As you think, you vibrate. And it is your vibrational offering that equals your point of attraction. So it's always a match. What you are thinking and what is coming back to you is always a vibrational match. The emotion (your Guidance System) is telling you what's coming."[19] and "...neither the good feeling you find when you observe wanted behavior, nor the bad feeling you find when you observe unwanted behavior, is actually the reason that you feel good or bad. The way you feel is only ever about your alignment, or misalignment, with the Source within you. It is only your relationship with the Source within you (with your own *Higher Self*) that is the reason for the emotions that you feel." And "Understanding that the way you feel is really about your relationship with your *Higher Self*, with the expanded version of you—gives you complete empowerment and absolute freedom."

In *The Happiness Hypothesis*, Jonathan Haidt shared research that clearly demonstrated that we cannot make a decision without emotion. In studies of individuals whose brains were damaged in ways that made it impossible for them to feel emotion, even simple decisions such as what they want to eat or drink become impossible. Our emotions give us information about what we want and what we do not want. We use that information every time we make a decision. The concept of a rational, Spock-like brain[20] that completely disregards emotion is a myth.

In some versions of the Bible, Proverbs 16:9 states "The mind of man plans his way, But the LORD directs his steps." In another version, it states, "The heart of man plans his way, But God directs his steps."

It does not say:

God guides your steps **if** you have established a relationship with God in your own life.

God guides your steps **if** you have opened communication channels between yourself and God.

God guides your steps **if** you are worthy of guidance.

God guides your steps **after** you've done sufficient good works to earn guidance from God.

It states that God guides <u>every</u> step.

This is not an empty promise. Every thought we think receives an emotional response from our Higher Self, or, as some would say, God. That response provides us with a clear reading on the relationship between where we want to go (what our heart wants) and the direction we are currently heading.

If our thought supports our desires, the emotional response feels good. If our thought contradicts our desires, the emotional response feels bad. If the thought is more in line with our desires than the preceding thought, we will feel a sense of relief (even if the thought still feels bad). An example of this would be moving from despair to anger. Anger feels better than despair, but is still not the feeling we want to feel. Interested feels pretty good, but passion feels even better and comes with a sense of relief when someone is moving from interested. There is literally no end to how good we can feel. There are emotional responses that provide relief from joy. Humans don't have words for those emotions, but it is possible to attain those emotional heights.[21]

The main reason humanity seems to be in such a mess is that we are all taught to misread our Emotional Guidance. The feeling of fear, for example, does not validate the thought and mean the perspective that elicits the feeling of fear is the best perspective we could have on that topic—but most think the fear means there is a reason to feel that way. The truth is, fear in most instances, is merely one's guidance communicating that the perspective taken on the subject is nowhere near the best perspective one could take on that particular subject. The only time a feeling of fear is accurate is when it is accompanied by the physical symptoms such as the hair standing up on the back of one's neck. Somehow, far back in time, humanity merged two completely different experiences and now behaves as if they are the same.

If the person who hears something on the news that makes her feel fear does not change her perspective, she flows energy toward what she doesn't want—the fearful situation she is imagining. But someone who understands what their Emotional Guidance is indicating will not do that. The person who understands how to use Emotional Guidance will recognize the emotion of fear as a sign that there is a better perspective on the topic that leads more directly to the fulfillment of her desires and use her mind to identify and adopt a better-feeling perspective.

Let's take the example of a newscast broadcasting a heinous crime. If the viewer watches that and worries that the same could happen to him, the feeling of fear is felt. The likelihood of the same crime happening to the viewer is very remote. I saw some research that showed that 1 in 1.5 million children are abducted, yet many parents live in almost daily fear that it could happen to their child.[22] The 1 in 1.5 million odds seems too large of a risk. This particular article indicated a way to greatly lessen the unreasonable fear of parents. Skanazy calculated that you would have to leave a child outside unattended for 750 years before you could be assured the child would be abducted. When it was put that way, it was easier for parents to let go of this fear. Managing risk is not wrong, but fear that one's efforts may not be successful is counterproductive.

If someone watches a newscast about the heinous crime and feels fear, the first thing to do is ask oneself what thought preceded the feeling of fear. Most likely it was fear that the same would happen to the viewer or a loved one of the viewer. By acknowledging the thought that led to fear, the person can recognize that the chances are highly unlikely and find more soothing thoughts such as, "This type of thing is rare and the chances of it happening to me are so slight I should not give it another thought." Or, another way to address it is by reminding yourself that you manage your risks. "I am not out walking the streets alone at night so I'd never be in the situation that led to that." If the crime happened at home there are multiple ways to reassure yourself that it is unlikely to happen to you. From reminding yourself that you live in a safe neighborhood, that you light the exterior of your home, that you lock your doors, that you have protection in the house, or just that you're not the type of person such things happen to.

Personally, if I am inadvertently where I can hear or see the news, I remind myself that the job of the media is to get good ratings and they know scaring us makes us more likely to watch.[23] The actual thought one finds is less important than how the thought feels. The point is that another perspective that feels better than the one that elicits fear can be found. Your guidance provides you with an emotional response to each thought you consider so you always know if your new thought is better or worse for you. Better feels better, worse feels worse. It is truly that simple.

Your guidance is fully aware of all your goals, including goals pertaining to things like maintaining good relationships and being kind to others, as well as being successful and happy. Your guidance knows what you want, "Man's heart plans..." but God (using Emotional Guidance) guides every step of the way.

When an individual is in a low emotional state, their cognitive abilities constrict.[24] They literally cannot think of solutions that may be readily apparent to an observer who is not at a low emotional state. In that state of more limited cognitive capacity, justifying an unsavory route to achieve one's goals (or perceived necessities) becomes far more likely.[25] Baumeister and Beck examined evil from the perspective of both victim and perpetrator in *Evil: Inside Human Cruelty and Aggression.*[26] When taking the perpetrator's perspective, they found that people who do things we see as evil, from spousal abuse all the way to genocide, rarely think they are doing anything wrong. *"They almost always see themselves as responding to attacks and provocations in ways that are justified."* [27, 28]

In Appendix I, there is an Emotional Guidance Scale (EGSc) in which emotions are separated into zones. The better-feeling emotions are at the top (higher) part of the scale. The lower one moves down the scale, the worse the emotional state. Zones are similar emotional states grouped together to ease discussion.[29]

In higher emotional states, the person will see more solutions. Someone who understands they have guidance and how to interpret it never dips very low on the emotional scale because knowing they have the guidance keeps them in the vicinity of hopefulness. Only when one's guidance is an enigma does one decline into lower emotional states. The lower one goes on the Emotional Guidance Scale, the worse behaviors a person is capable of justifying in her mind.

Emotional Guidance is so easy to understand we could teach it to kindergarteners. It is a bit more difficult to teach it to adults (because they've learned more false premises that have to be overturned) but large groups can be taught to understand and use their Emotional Guidance with amazing benefits. The size of the group being taught does not matter because one-on-one work is not necessary with the majority of the audience. The best one-on-one work occurs between each individual and their own emotional feedback.

I've personally worked with groups between 60 and 260 individuals who have achieved results such as:

- Overcoming suicidal ideation and finding a stable positive emotional stance
- Releasing anger toward everyone in their life
- Increasing resilience
- Being freed from the bondage created when one attempts to please someone who (due to a low emotional state) is unpleasable and the resultant low self-esteem that results from that Sisyphus type challenge.[30]

- Improved relationships of all types
- Achieving increasingly more positive perspectives about life and one's personal circumstances
- Overcoming PTSD and over 30 years of suffering
- Healthier Self-esteem
- Stronger internal locus of control
- Increased levels of happiness
- Decreased levels of stress

The research is very clear that individuals who are more positively focused are kinder to others, including strangers.[31] In one study, a man of the cloth walked over someone who needed help after researchers primed him with a negative mood and a time constraint for his task. Negative emotional states restrict our thought-action repertoire making us overlook opportunities to help that we would respond to when in a more positive mindset.[32] Researchers repeatedly find that positively focused individuals are more likely to offer help and provide more assistance than negatively focused individuals. The research is also very clear that happy individuals are less likely to commit crimes.[33] Additional research reveals that behaviors such as drinking to excess and drug abuse are usually the result of unmanaged stress.[34] An understanding of one's Emotional Guidance greatly reduces stress and increases resilience. Alcohol[35] and drug abuse[36] often lead to crime.

When stress (a significant root cause of drug abuse) is reduced the results include: reduced drug and alcohol abuse, increases life satisfaction, and reduction in crime. The cause of the stress does not matter. The stress may be the result of low self-esteem, financial worries, relationship worries, peer pressure, high demands, poverty, environment, abuse, perceived discrimination, experiences, or any other cause. Emotional Guidance provides guidance in all areas of life—no area is ignored. An individual with low self-esteem who learns to understand and trust her guidance will quickly recognize how bogus thoughts of unworthiness are based on the response from her Emotional Guidance. Bogus became one of my favorite words when I learned about my guidance because it was so thrilling to receive the positive emotional response when I called such thoughts bogus. It was clear my guidance agreed derisive thoughts about me were bogus.

In a study of foster children, stress was linked to increased criminal activities. Low self-esteem was a major contributor to stress and increased criminal activity.[37] "Threatened self-esteem accounts for a large portion of violence at the individual level…"[38] Sylvia Browne spoke of the common habit of low self-esteem in *The Nature of Good and Evil*, "We don't construct a large enough God, outside or inside. We walk around underestimating our Source, with poor self-esteem, not knowing who we are, where we have been, where we're going, and what we should do."[39]

Emotional Guidance can be used to stabilize and increase self-esteem to healthy levels without requiring anyone else to validate the thoughts that support self-worth. One way Merriam-Webster defines offend is "to cause a person to feel hurt, angry, or upset by something said or done." I've personally found that using my guidance has stabilized my self-esteem to the point where it seems impossible to offend me. I simply do not give others the power to offend my sensibilities.

When I find another's actions morally offensive, such as someone asking me to do something I view as unethical, I do not take it as something the person has considered, such as "Is Jeanine unethical enough to participate in this?" Instead, I view it as their lack of critical and evaluative thinking about the topic. It's not personal to me, so it does not offend me. For example someone recently asked me to attend a breakfast meeting at a hotel where they serve complimentary breakfast to guests but do not have menus or a method whereby non-guests can reimburse the hotel for the meal. To my view, attending and eating would be unethical and I refused to participate in the meeting at that location. I did not feel offended that he thought I would participate. I don't think he gave the ethics of what he was asking any thought, much less that he made a conscious judgment about my ethics.

I could have justified joining the meeting at the hotel. I have stayed at that same hotel chain many times and not had the free breakfast that was offered. I could have used that to justify partaking because *they owed me* for the times when I stayed there and did not eat. But that just seemed to be an argument to make my perspective feel better—not one that was fully valid. Nor did I judge harshly the ethics of the individual who proposed the meeting. His focus was on expediency, not evaluating the ethics of the situation.

My guidance highlights ethical situations because I reinforce my personal goal of being ethical and because I spent many years in a role that required me to be continually conscious of the ethics of situations I encountered. That makes both my guidance and my mind highlight such situations. Are there situations where I miss the mark? I'm sure there are—but never on purpose. Just as the host who invited me to the meeting was not consciously aware of how the venue was perceived, my hubris is not such that I believe I am always of all the factors that affect every perspective from which any situation can be perceived.

What I do know is that I, and everyone else, can learn when they make a mistake and adjust their filters so the filters will be more helpful in future situations.

I also find that in the last few years people will often say, "I'm sorry if I've offended you." in both personal conversations and written communications. Although I admit I don't spend a lot of time trying to figure out how they could have offended me, it's not obvious with a cursory glance. Oftentimes, it is someone who claims to have been teasing me. Sometimes it is someone who is arguing against my position. I guess those who argue against another's position may be found offensive by those whose ego is tied to others agreeing with their position. If their goal is discourse and deeper understanding, I do not believe they are offended by other viewpoints. If they understand that everyone has a different perception, then they would not be offended simply because they learn of another's viewpoint.

I attribute my lack of *offendability* to using my Emotional Guidance.

Financial worries never seem as bad when you understand your guidance. You understand that paying attention to the guidance will lead you to the answers you need or to the people you need to meet. It helps you maintain a hopeful Emotional State, which keeps your mind open to opportunities that justify your hope and help you recover from an adverse situation.

Your guidance is pure gold with respect to creating the relationships you want in your life. It lets you know who uplifts you through their presence and whose company lowers your energy level. It helps you maintain the type of relationships you desire. Your guidance will let you know whom to trust and whom to avoid. As you maintain increasingly higher emotional states—your relations become closer and it is easier to broach subjects that you avoided the in the past. New people may come into your life because your positive Emotional State is attractive to others who are positively focused in ways a negatively focused person is not. Negative people in your life may begin spending less time with you or they may be inspired to learn more about how you're managed to shift the trajectory of your life.

High demands from others often increase stress levels, but that is because we are not here to please others. It goes back to the fact that when we selfishly take care of ourselves first, we have far more to give. If our needs are not met, we have nothing to give another anyway. Our guidance will lead us to a perspective that serves us. When we act from love, we do not do favors for our loved ones. When we act from love, we do things for our loved ones because the things we do support the relationship we desire.

When we *do favors*, scorekeeping can take place and that does not serve the relationship. When we do things for others because we *should*, resentment can build over time. When we selfishly do what we do because it nurtures and feeds the relationships we want, there is no scorekeeping or resentment. When I cook dinner for my husband, I do it because it pleases me to do so. If it does not please me to do so on any particular evening, I don't do it. I do nothing out of obligation. Even in our wedding vows, we stated emphatically that there are many different types of relationships from which to choose and we freely choose to be monogamous because that is our desire. This vow came from a desire each of us holds to have that type of relationship. Contrast this to the societal expectation that marriage demands monogamy. If your eyes are open, you will see that many marriages do not include monogamy—some with full agreement between the partners for some variation of polyamory and some in which subterfuge is at play. Decisions have power.

On an energetic level, I felt strongly that there was a significant difference between consciously and deliberately choosing monogamy vs. having the expectation of monogamy thrust upon us just because that is what society expects marriage agreements to include. Even though we desire a traditional style of relationship, acknowledging we were consciously making that choice felt far better to us. We made a decision.

Katherine Peil's groundbreaking work on emotions as guidance states, "They reflect the self-regulatory feedback dynamics—and epigenetic manifestations of the emotional sense."[40] Emotions are guidance. They let us know whether we are moving in the direction of becoming more like our *Higher Self* (feels better) or away from whom we have decided we want to be (feels worse). Think of it as the children's game where they find a hidden object where clues of *you're getting warmer* or *you're getting colder* are given and it becomes simple to follow our guidance.[41]

Earlier I stated positive emotions mean we are moving in the right direction and negative emotions indicate we are moving away from our goal, but what is the **right** direction? It depends. Your guidance is morally relative. An individual's moral code "...involves being disposed to act in certain ways and to feel a certain range of emotions. For instance, if someone sincerely accepts a moral norm prohibiting gossip, then that person is disposed to avoid engaging in gossip. Moreover, such a person who knowingly violates the norm in question is likely to experience feelings of guilt or perhaps shame as a proper response to the violation."[42]

> *Helpful Hint:*
>
> *It's very natural to want to help our friends and family feel better when we learn how, but it is best to teach by example.*
> *I've found that the more you stay quiet about what you're doing until you're asked, the more open old friends to the information you share. If you try to encourage them to do what you're doing before they are ready they can become resistant, which delays (and sometimes prevents) their interest.*

It is important to remember that the moral norms, what is considered right and wrong by a given society, change over time. Not all individuals' morality changes at the same pace as that of society. Individual moral norms can also change during life as the result of experience, insight, enlightenment, or other events.

When you look at every paradigm shift there are those who lead the change, sharing their insights and ideas. The leaders are often ridiculed. Napoleon Hill wrote *Outwitting the Devil: The Secret to Freedom and Success* decades before it was published because the ideas and concepts presented were so revolutionary his family and friend feared the backlash that might ensue.

Early adopters, on the other hand, have become wealthy by using knowledge that most people are not yet willing to accept. Then we have those who been come to be called sheepeople in the Urban Dictionary, the ones who follow whatever the crowd thinks and believes, without deciding for themselves what is best for themselves. They have the most to gain by learning to understand and use their guidance.

Understanding our relationship to our *Higher Self* helps us to understand why this Hindu Proverb is so true:

There is nothing noble about being superior to some other man. The true nobility is in being superior to your prior self.

The Ought Self

This *Ideal Self* or *Higher Self* is different from the *Ought Self* that is the construct of things we believe that we **should** or **ought** to do based on expectations and requirements of others.

The *Ideal Self* or *Higher Self* motivates us from within. The *Ought Self* is using external criteria to motivate and may or may not be in alignment with our true goals.

What is the difference between our *Ideal Self* or *Higher Self* and who we usually are in our day to day interactions? The **gap** between who we are being and our *Ideal Self* has a lot to do with what we believe we are capable of being. There is always a gap because the *Ideal Self* or *Higher Self* is a moving target and this is a good thing. Some of the greatest athletes of all time focused on moving toward their *Ideal Self* or *Higher Self* and continued to improve even when they were great. The *Ideal Self* or *Higher Self* is a self-created self that is the best we ever imagined being at any time. As long as we are moving in a direction that is closing the gap we can feel joyful.

Take the idea of the *Ideal Self* or *Higher Self* and then look at the Emotional Guidance Scale (EGSc) in Appendix I. You will easily be able to see that the *Ideal Self* or *Higher Self* calls everyone up the EGSc. Our *Ideal Self* or *Higher Self* lives at the high end of the scale, loving and appreciating.

You will also see that the higher we go on the scale the more empowered we feel. The lower we are on the scale the more powerless we feel.

When we feel more empowered we see many paths to our goals (which is why science has found that individuals are more creative and intelligent when they are happier—their happiness reflects a greater belief in their abilities). Therefore, they see more ways to achieve their goals. When someone is held down, either by society or his or her own limiting beliefs, the pull to regain some power and to move up the scale gets stronger. When the only path(s) that are visible to the individual are ones that society abhors, they will take those paths if and when that pull becomes stronger than any resistance they have to those actions.

Understanding this relationship is the key to seeing the importance of changing the way we commonly respond to undesired behaviors.

Impact of Emotional State

An individual's current emotional state has significant impacts on all of the following:

Behavior	Intelligence	Emotional Intelligence
Health	Well-being	Resilience
Relationships	Motivation	Creativity

Decisions (including lifestyle, i.e., diet, exercise, alcohol, drugs, and risky behavior)

In general, one can assume that someone behaving in undesirable ways has negative emotions that have not been responded to in one of the three constructive methods.

The best response to most negative emotion in modern society involves *Right Responses* (RRs).[43] RRs involve some action or a deliberate and conscious change in the mindscape.[44] When an individual does not understand how to change their perspective to effect a better-feeling emotional response, downward spirals can result. The negative emotion leads to bad behavior, which leads to worsening relationships, which reinforces the negative emotional states and creates a circle that is difficult to break out of unless the individual knows they have emotional guidance.

Emotions provide information to guide us. The other two appropriate responses are Fight (non-violent assertive resistance) or Flight.[45] Suppressing or denying emotions is dysfunctional and leads to many other problems.

Ignoring a negative emotion is just as unhealthy as putting your hand on a hot stove and leaving it there to burn while attempting to ignore the pain inflicted.[46] Pain is information that tells us to take some action. Likewise, emotions are guidance that helps us recognize unhealthy thoughts or circumstances.

If we are judging an unhappy person based on their behavior, we are not seeing their potential. When we see their potential, we are more likely to inspire them to achieve more of their potential. Potential is a terrible thing to waste.

Violent criminals sometimes appear happy at their own actions, but what is being witnessed is a sense of relief they feel in moving up the Emotional Guidance Scale to a more empowered Emotional State from somewhere in the vicinity of despair (which feels totally powerless) to somewhere like revenge, where some of their power has been taken back. Their seemingly positive emotion is not joy, appreciation, or love. They are just reflecting a feeling of relief—which is always present when we move up the EGSc.

It is not necessary to commit violent acts in order to move up through the Hot (red) Zone (See Appendix I) and stabilize at higher emotional set points. In fact, violence does not usually happen until a person has tried to move up and been repeatedly thwarted in their more socially acceptable attempts to feel better, such as a child who tries to tell her mom about abuse and is not believed.

Society finds depressed individuals easier to deal with than angry ones. Without understanding that anger is on the path between depression and joy we often push people back to depression. It is quite possible to move up from despair and hopelessness through anger, rage, and revenge just using thoughts. Actions are not necessary to move up the scale. A guide or friend who also understands this process is often helpful.

It may seem that I am blaming those who have held others down or pushed them back down for their resulting violent behaviors. In actuality, I am not interested in trying to figure out who is to blame. Someone taught the person that pushed them back down beliefs that punishing them and limiting his or her power was the right way to act and the person who taught them learned it from another and so on back through time. Attempting to discern the beginning is not the highest and best use of our time and efforts.

Being in a positive state of mind increases social engagement that then creates resources that help the individual when adversities arise. Three leading psychology researchers noted that "When all is going well, a person is not well served by withdrawing into a self-protective stance in which the primary aim is to protect his or her existing resources and to avoid harm—a process marking the experience of negative emotions."[47]

Emotions and Thoughts

That emotions are responses to thoughts is easily demonstrated by taking someone through a guided visualization of scenes designed to elicit emotions. As the scene changes, the emotional state changes.

There are actually three levels of emotions. The most basic level responds below the level of conscious thought. For example, the hairs on the back of your neck standing up because of a danger you have not yet consciously noticed.

The second level consists of simple emotions that come in response to an actual thought. Frustration is one such emotion.

The third level is also composed of emotions that come as the result of conscious thoughts, but the thoughts are more complex, and the responses are not necessarily inborn responses, but trained by external third parties (parents, religion, society, teachers, etc.). Shame is an example of a complex emotion. Babies and small children do not feel shame about their bodies when they are naked. This emotion is taught by third parties and is a complex negative emotion.[48]

Emotions provide information that we are designed to act upon. When third-party-imposed negative emotions do not provide a path to better feeling emotions, they set the stage for all sorts of problems, including behavioral, emotional,[49] and health. We were not designed to suffer negative emotions on a long-term basis and, when we endure them, we do suffer—physical, mental, and behavioral health and emotional pain.

We were never designed to tolerate negative emotions for longer than it takes to complete our corrective action, which is usually a Right Response, a simple change of perception. That is why the many benefits of positivity are coming to light as we study positive emotions. We were designed to feel good. We were also designed to be good, which we are when we feel good.

Societal systems designed to make us feel bad and maintain negative emotional states are fighting against our very nature. These systems literally create the undesired behaviors we want to avoid.

Right Responses can be an individual's default response in most stressful situations. Stress can be defined as not moving in the direction of our *Higher* or *Ideal Self.* When we move away from our *Higher* or *Ideal Self,* the stress level is even higher. Think of it like a tug of war. If everyone holding onto the rope is moving in the same direction, there is no stress. If one person is holding the rope so the other side cannot back up, there is tension (stress) in the rope. If one person is pulling on the rope so that it moves in opposition to the direction the others are pulling, there is increasing stress.

Emotional Guidance System Uses

There is a human tendency to believe we are only capable of those things which we are aware another has achieved. The most commonly cited example of this is the 4-minute mile that was once considered impossible for a human. As soon as someone was recorded breaking the 4-minute mile barrier several other runners did the same. Our belief in our ability to achieve something is a limiting or expanding factor in our personal ability to achieve it. Henry Ford said, "Whether you believe you can or you believe you can't, either way you're right." His words remain one of the clearest expressions of this concept of which I'm aware.

Your *Higher Self* says "Yes, You can" which you can verify by thinking (and believing) "I can" and feeling your emotional response to the thought. Your emotional response will feel better than it will when you think and feel "I can't" The potential our guidance gives us is far more empowering than awareness someone else was able to accomplish something. Once one has used their guidance on a regular basis and come to trust it, Emotional Guidance can be used to deliberately shore up a belief in our personal ability to achieve something that no one else has ever achieved. Our guidance will provide positive feedback encouraging us to reach for our dreams and will highlight ideas that support those goals. It becomes unnecessary to know someone else who has achieved what we wish to achieve before we can do it. We can get our sureness from our Emotional Guidance.

Years ago when I read a short biography about Andrew Carnegie who grew up in poverty but repeatedly said from a young age that he would grow up to be wealthy so he could take care of his Mum. Many would say that a young boy with his lowly beginnings could not achieve what he achieved. His success is partly because he developed a belief (a thought you think repeatedly until you believe it)[50] that he could and would. But I guarantee that each time he stated the affirmation that he would grow up and become wealthy so he could take care of his Mum, his Emotional Guidance encouraged him in that assertion.

Those living in or growing up in poverty today can use their Emotional Guidance in the same way Andrew Carnegie did nearly a century ago. In the environment that exists today, it is more likely that the belief that the only way out of their circumstances is sports will be developed, but their guidance will tell them that this is bogus. There are millions of potential paths to a better future and their guidance will guide them to the path that suits their unique goals, dreams, and desires—if they are aware of it.

Understanding one's Emotional Guidance is the absolutely best method of stress relief available. It is free, easy to use, 100% reliable, and has the benefit of broader perspective. Emotional Guidance is supported by science.[51] In addition to being supported by science, Emotional Guidance is also supported by the holy books of many religious persuasions:

Proverbs 3:5 "Trust in the Lord with all your heart and lean not on your own understanding; In all your ways acknowledge Him, and He will make your paths straight."

Proverbs 16:9 "A man's heart plans his way, but the Lord directs his steps" seems to echo exactly that the guidance is specific to our unique goals.

Neither the science nor the various religious worldviews about guidance are necessary for any individual to understand, use, and trust his or her own guidance. The reason is because once one becomes aware that emotions are guidance and begins understanding how to accurately interpret their guidance, the guidance itself proves its value in each life.

In fact, most people who have lived a bit of life can look back at their past experiences, overlaying their new understanding of Emotional Guidance and see that they were receiving it but that they simply misinterpreted their emotions because they had been taught that it meant something different.

The Bible is far from the only holy book that points to guidance. Examples from other belief structures include:

From the **Bhagwath Gita**:

"The Supersoul within everyone's heart, directly gives us guidance...the spiritual master in the heart, gives direct inspiration."

From **The Koran (Al-Qur'an)**:

"By this the reader will observe that the Mohammedans are no strangers to Quietism. Others, however, understand the words of the soul, which, having attained the knowledge of the truth, rests satisfied, and relies securely thereon, undisturbed by doubts; or of the soul which is secure of its salvation, and free from fear or sorrow."

If this passage does not resonate with you, come back to it after using your guidance for a while. The absence of both fear and sorrow are brought about by following one's guidance when consciously determining which thoughts to believe.

From **Śrīmad-Bhāgavatam**:

"The Lord's mercy is therefore available both in the form of the instructing spiritual masters and the Supersoul within the heart."

From **Tao**:

1. Without going outside his door, one understands (all that takes place) under the sky; without looking out from his window, one sees the Tao of Heaven. The farther that one goes out (from himself), the less he knows. 2. Therefore the sages got their knowledge without travelling; gave their (right) names to things without seeing them; and accomplished their ends without any purpose of doing so.

From **Buddhist teachings**:

"Wisdom is born of meditation deep, But lost by mind's distraction; knowing these Two paths of loss and gain, so let him live, Let him so direct his life that wisdom may increase."

From **Confucius**:

"By three methods we may learn wisdom: first, by reflection, which is noblest; second, by imitation, which is easiest; and third, by experience, which is the most bitter."

Similar wisdom is found in other belief structures. I would encourage anyone who feels concern about the use of emotional guidance conflicting with religious beliefs to explore the teachings of their religion for indications that suggest guidance is available. For those who have chosen to live according to religious beliefs, I suggest the correlations are strong enough to allow room for Emotional Guidance to be incorporated into their existing religious beliefs and practices. The examples are far from the only passages in holy books that point to guidance. Finding passages in such divergent books makes it seem universal, something I would have found encouraging if I was not already sure that my guidance increased my ability to thrive.

Non-Religious and Non-Spiritual View

The absolute beauty of our guidance systems, the brilliance of its design, is that a belief in God is not required for the system to work perfectly. Following the guidance by paying attention to what feels better and using Right Responses in response to emotional guidance leads us to lives of thriving regardless of our religious or spiritual beliefs or the absence thereof.

Positive emotions are so beneficial for us — increasing our resilience, reducing the risks from negative life events, decreasing the risk of all types of major illnesses and improving relationships.[52] We have Emotional Guidance that helps us enjoy better-feeling emotions. It makes sense to use the guidance available to us.

Crime and Punishment

I am not advocating opening the doors of the prisons and emptying their contents back into society, rather I am advocating providing knowledge and skills to every member of society (incarcerated or not) that enables each individual to manage his or her own emotional state to a high level, thus greatly reducing their likelihood of committing crimes. However, believing we can punish people into better behavior is not the only flaw in the current system. Science is well aware of flaws that are caused by psychological processes in the individuals involved in the criminal justice system.

"Our focus is not on intentional wrongdoing; we assume that all the players in the system are generally trying to achieve an accurate and just result. Rather, we are interested in the ways honest and well-intentioned decision makers go astray, and how to counteract the common psychological tendencies that can undermine even the best intentions."[53]

Despite the above-mentioned good intentions, this study found that mistakes are commonly made. The eyewitness that the general public seems to believe is so reliable is one of the least reliable sources of evidence. Again, this is not due to conscious decisions or dishonesty on the part of the witness—it is more evidence that our society does not understand how their own minds work, the filters (biases) through which each individual perceives reality, or how underlying beliefs and expectations impact our perception and backstory.

On the surface, factors that contribute to criminal behavior are as distinct as the individuals involved. When one looks deeper it becomes apparent that emotional state is a significant contributing factor to the behavior. Digging further still, one sees that stress, specifically unmanaged stress, is a systemic issue that leads to the low emotional states. In 2010, The Institute of Child Development at the University of Minnesota undertook a study that found common predictors of future crime by adult males included AFDC (Aid to Families with Dependent Children) participation by the child's age 3, negative early home environment, maltreatment experiences between ages 4 – 13, and the number of school moves between ages 10-14.[54, 55] Other research has demonstrated repeatedly that abuse (verbal, physical, and sexual) greatly increase the likelihood of adverse behavioral, physical, and mental health.

Research demonstrates that children taught skills that develop resilience and healthy self-esteem are far more likely to avoid the undesired outcomes.

The techniques suggested herein will improve the behaviors offered by both sides of the law enforcement paradigm (suspects/criminals and enforcement personnel).

The False Premise of Good and Evil

The belief that some people are *good* and others are *evil* is so prevalent in our society it is accepted unquestioned by most despite copious evidence to the contrary. For centuries, a concept called the Great Chain of Being has been used to rank the value of beings, from lowest to highest. Demons have held the lowest rank with Gods holding the top and humans residing somewhere between the two. This concept can be found in science, theology, and various schools of philosophy. At the lower ends, dehumanization is common and at the upper end, deification or sanctification.[56] This Great Chain of Being is further divided with some humans being considered subhuman, or *evil*, as the result of their behavior (or due to the other labels constructed by man).

To dispel this belief we have to look at the effect of emotional stance on behavior. We can begin at home. Almost everyone has experienced a bad day and been grouchy when loved ones came home in the evening. When this happens, we are far more likely to say things we later regret, we are less likely to see the positive aspects in others, we are more likely to pick fights with those we love the most, and we are more likely to be unkind.

There is also, in each individual life, examples of times when our behavior was less than we wanted it to be because we felt bad, or were depleted from a lack of rest or insufficient food. Anyone who is honest with him or herself will admit his or her behavior varies with mood and that a good mood elicits better behaviors. The range differs from individual to individual. Someone who is highly advanced spiritually may simply withdraw until he feels better, recognizing the need of body or mind for rest, respite, or re-centering. Someone not quite as advanced might not withdraw physically but will refrain from voicing the unkind words that he would have said before he learned a better way. Another person, less aware of one's ability to consciously manage emotional state, might lash out with words, fists, or adulterous behavior when he is in a bad mood or reach for alcohol or drugs to dampen the unwelcome emotional state.

When we are grouchy, we treat others in ways we'd never behave when we are happy. This common example shows that mood affects behavior. The rest is simply a matter of degree.

Look at the profiling information for criminals.[57] In every instance, the worst ones are assumed to have horrid events in their past. The perspective an individual takes about his or her past has a direct influence on how adverse the effects become on future life experience. A child who is repeatedly abused may become abusive or even a serial killer. Another child who was repeatedly abused may appreciate that she knows how strong she is because she lived through those experiences and work tirelessly to help others recover and thrive. The difference is not that one is *good* and the other *evil*. The difference is the perspective the child and later, the adult, takes regarding the experiences. Perspective is a choice, but most people believe the first perspective they have about any situation is the truth—never realizing the power they could wield by choosing a perspective that feels better. We all have the ability to literally change the past by perceiving it differently.

Watch any law enforcement show and in every case the *bad* person has a history that led to his or her current undesired behavior. Occasionally, there is someone who appears to have been a *bad seed,* but in every one of those circumstances, you learn that those around the child expected bad from the child. Expectation influences behavior on the quantum level with practiced beliefs having a more dominant effect. In every situation, if sufficient information is obtained, there are valid and scientifically explainable reasons why the individual exhibited even the most horrendous undesirable behaviors. There are no inherently *evil* people. There are simply people who have experienced situations that made them feel bad or disempowered and perspectives they maintained that did not serve their highest good. Those perspectives created negative emotional states,[58] which exacerbated the situation by constricting cognitive processes[59] and immune function.[60]

Overwhelming research demonstrates that early life experiences such as abuse, maternal depression, maltreatment, poverty, family adversity, violence, and other stressors are linked with physical, mental, and behavioral health problems in children and the adults they become.[61]

If we believe in a Source or God or *Higher Power* with infinite abilities, how can we reconcile such an entity with a child who is born *evil*? The two are, in my opinion, mutually exclusive. Neither can the form of something be changed from *good* to *evil*. If something is comprised of *good*, it does not have the capacity to change form to *evil*. There is great evidence, in the scientific research and in each of our individual lives, that behavior is largely based on chronic and current mood with the better mood eliciting better behavior. Yet society responds to bad behavior in ways that further reduce the mood of transgressors. We ignore that the reason for the transgressions is the existence of a low mood or low chronic emotional state.

It is no wonder that crime has been steadily increasing decade after decade. It is no wonder that crime increases when the economy plummets.[62]

The relationship between behavior and mood is evident, but the belief that some nebulous *evil* aspect of personality, genetics, or fate is responsible keeps our eyes averted from the truth—and the solutions that are available to us when we recognize the truth. We blind ourselves to the solutions and the root cause by pointing at a non-existent figment of imagination (*evil*). This is not a truth that requires extensive research. There is sufficient research linking happiness to lower crime and unhappiness to crime to satisfy the most discerning analyst.

I am not saying that *evil* behavior does not exist. I am saying that people are not *evil*.

For example, Jeffrey Dahmer, a notorious serial killer was neglected by both parents at a young age, subjected to considerable tension in his childhood home topped by his parents' divorce his senior year in high school. Jeffrey had turned 18, so his parents did not have a custody battle over him as they did his younger brother and left Jeffrey living alone in the family home without food or money.[63] Despite the fact that the courts did not have jurisdiction over custody of a child who was 18, in the mind of someone who already felt rejected, their failure to fight for custody of him could have increased his sense of rejection. Add to that the fact that he was left in the family home without food or money and you have a very hurt young man.

Various accounts of Dahmer's history indicate that although he was given little attention, when he expressed curiosity about dead animals, his scientist father perceived it as scientific curiosity and encouraged his interest. He was also homosexual at a time when that created far more turmoil than today (1978). At his trial he was considered to have Borderline Personality Disorder (BPD) defined as "A pervasive pattern of instability of interpersonal relationships, self-image, and affects, and marked impulsivity that begins by early adulthood and is present in a variety of contexts."[64] Dahmer had developed several diagnosable illnesses, including Alcohol Abuse Disorder from heavy drinking that began when he was 14, which he referred to as *his medicine* when a classmate asked him why he was drinking at school.

Stacey Lannert killed her father while he was asleep on a sofa. Her father had begun abusing her when she was 8, first raped her when she was 9, and became especially violent and abusive when he drank. Her reason for killing her father was to protect her younger sister from further abuse. Lannert felt disempowered and could not conceive of another way to protect her younger sister. She had attempted to tell her mother and a babysitter about the abuse when she was younger and, lacking adequate language, was unable to make them understand. This failed attempt might have led her to believe that telling would not solve the problem. "Violence may seem to be the only option to remove the threat." David Winter wrote in *Construing the Construction Processes of Serial Killers and Other Violent Offenders.*[65]

Charles Manson claims to have a single happy childhood memory, that of the woman who gave birth to him at the age of 16 hugging him upon her release from jail when he was eight years old. She later abandoned and rejected him when he attempted to rejoin her. His father was a transient and it is unknown if Manson ever met him. His given name on his birth certificate was no-name.[66]

Childhood trauma does not excuse bad behavior, but it does create it—in some individuals. Not every child who is neglected, raped, abandoned, or abused becomes a criminal. What is the difference between those who do and those who do not? It is not an inherent *goodness* or *evil*. It is how resilient the child is. If the child can find and maintain emotional states that prevent him or her from taking that path, the child is more likely to lead a productive and even happy life.

"Strains such as unemployment, school exclusion, length of time in care and instability of placement were significant predictors of involvement in criminal activity among foster youth. Conditioning factors, namely self-esteem and life skills acquired prior to leaving care, tend to mediate the relationship between these strains and criminal involvement... *Providing children with skills that enable them to reduce the amount of stress they experience in response to life events beyond their control reduces the cumulative effect of stress, thus reducing the likelihood of developing aggressive tendencies.*" [67] (Emphasis added)

Could understanding Emotional Guidance prevent outcomes like these? We won't know until we try. If we don't try, we'll never know. When one understands his guidance, he is led to thoughts that feel better about the circumstances in life and to inspired actions that lead to the best possible outcome. The parent who abandons a child needs the benefit of guidance as does the child. The parent who abandons a child would not do so if other, more empowered paths were perceivable to him or her. Understanding how to interpret guidance accurately provides the best chance of finding thoughts that will lead to the best outcome.

In *As a Man Thinketh*, James Allen wrote: "Man is made or unmade by himself; in the armoury of thought he forges the weapons by which he destroys himself; he also fashions the tools with which he builds for himself heavenly mansions of joy and strength and peace. By the right choice and true application of thought, man ascends to the Divine Perfection; by the abuse and wrong application of thought, he descends below the level of the beast. Between these two extremes are all the grades of character, and man is their maker and master." [68]

If our Emotional Guidance leads us to thoughts that create strength, peace and joy, can we not avoid the destruction of self brought about by unhealthy habits of thought? Could this not be true regardless of circumstances?

When a psychiatrist asked me how I had been so resilient back in 1995, I did not even know that I was more resilient than most that had lived my circumstances. Now I understand that I stumbled upon habits of thought that served me well. I was merely lucky. Today children can have this advantage without luck—if we act. My heart grieves for all the lives lived far below their potential because children did not figure this out on their own and for all those who continue to suffer even though the research points to a clear preventive measure that avoids emotional pain and suffering and empowers them to live the lives they were born to live, to be fully functioning, contributing members of society.

When society begins consciously recognizing that mood affects behavior and teaching skills that empower individuals to improve their mood and maintain True Happiness, crime rates will decline rapidly. The research is very clear that happy individuals are kinder and exhibit a greater willingness to help others—even complete strangers. The behaviors idealized in a Utopian society are present in happy individuals. Many happy people will readily admit that they selfishly help others feel better because it makes them feel so good when they uplift others.

At the lower levels of the Emotional Guidance Scale (EGSc), the only path visible that will allow the individual to regain some of their personal power is often a path that would never be chosen if they perceived a more desirable path as a possibility.

This answers the question of why most people cannot conceive of the actions some people take—because most people can see other potential paths. We will often second guess why a person did not seek help before he committed an abhorrent act. From the perspective held at the time the act was committed, he did not perceive a less destructive path that he believed would work.

If the individual had been taught skills and an understanding of how to feel emotionally better he would not be so low on the EGSc that the results of his decisions end up in the news. A society that understands the relationship between emotion and behavior will change their public policies, education system, and public service announcements to ensure that citizens understand and use their Emotional Guidance to achieve and sustain healthy emotional states.

The above point is so important to understand. Because of the feelings of being powerless the path(s) to regaining some power seem very limited when one is in a prolonged emotional state at the lowest ends of the EGSc. Perhaps they tried repeatedly to regain some power in more acceptable ways but have not been understood so they were pushed back down. Over time this results in a belief that more socially acceptable paths are not the way because they did not work—perhaps this happened to Stacy Lannert. As that happens repeatedly the paths that still seem open become more appealing to the individual. Paths that would never have been considered if the socially acceptable paths had not been blocked begin to seem like the only option. Feelings of desperation begin to work on the individual until it leads to actions. They do feel relief in those actions, even when the consequences are terrible.

When society begins helping individuals move from feelings of powerlessness to better-feeling places, rather than pushing them back down (because they are easier to handle in depression, despair, and helplessness than in anger or revenge) we will see broad-reaching positive changes in our crime rates. Eventually we will have the nice problem of trying to figure out what to do with excess capacity in our incarceration facilities.

We will see thriving among those who were once thought to have no hope. We will see children, whom today seem unable to achieve, begin to close the gap between who they have been and their *Ideal* or *Higher Self.*

Before we consciously accept that emotional state affects behavior we have to loosen our hold on the bogus concept that some humans are *evil.* We cling to the idea that there are *good* people and *evil* people because it helps us believe that if we do our best to be good, we won't be *evil*. The truth is that it is a sustained low emotional state (which may be because of their environment or because of their learned thought-processes) that leads to *evil* behavior—not an inherent attribute of the individual.

Emotional state can be managed with skills even children can learn. If everyone learned those skills very few people would live in low enough emotional states long enough to become a problem for society. Some factors make people more susceptible to low emotional states and criminal behavior. Emotional Guidance helps those individuals, too.

One flawed approach I am seeing recommended today is to target programs at those who need them because of discernable factors. The reason this is a misguided approach is that it is not just in poor homes that children are abused and abuse is a significant contributor to adverse outcomes. And, counter to common beliefs, verbal abuse often leads to the worst outcomes. The reasons for this are all countered by using emotional guidance. A child who understands her emotional guidance will know her mom's hurtful words that she is ugly are bogus. A child who understands his guidance will know that his father's taunts that he will never amount to anything are bogus.

It is also not just poor children who are bullied or who have physical characteristics that make childhood more difficult than it is for most.

Primary Prevention necessitates teaching every child (and as many adults as possible) about their guidance and how to use it. Just like it is easier to prevent illness by washing our hands than administering antibiotics intravenously in the hospital, it is easier to empower children with skills whether or not the need is apparent than to incarcerate them, or put them into drug and alcohol treatment programs.

Factors Contributing to Low Self-Esteem That Increase Crime

Morals and Values

Morals and values do have a place in the structure of things. Someone with strong moral fiber who is repeatedly pushed to the low end of the EGSc may choose options other than violence against others. Suicide is one of the options that can be more palatable to such an individual (slow or fast—in other words drugs and alcohol or those actions we refer to as suicide). There are so many variations that influence the path(s) that will become acceptable and there is really no reason to analyze them extensively. Time is much more productively spent understanding how to help individuals move up the EGSc where the subject of what path they would choose from a position of powerlessness is irrelevant. None of us are whom we want to be when we're at the low end of the Emotional Guidance Scale.

It is important to remember that our *Higher* or *Ideal Self* includes our desire for good relationships and to be liked, appreciated and of benefit to others. Our emotions will guide us in much better ways than the ego might to these goals.

Substance Abuse

In most cases, drug and alcohol abuse begins as a way to feel better. Individuals who know how to feel good by managing their own place on the EGSc tend to drink far less.

Drugs and alcohol are a form of self-medication, a response to stress. Whether addiction becomes an issue or not, learning to consciously and deliberately respond appropriately to one's Emotional Guidance can help any individual make healthier choices. The higher emotional state one sustains, the lower the risk for drug and alcohol abuse becomes. For those wishing to end an addiction, understanding Emotional Guidance will help prevent relapse via its stress reducing properties.

Peer Pressure

What about peer pressure? Think about it. The connection is easy to make. Isn't giving in to peer pressure an attempt to feel better? To reduce stress? To feel more accepted? To feel a part of something more?

Peer pressure is artificially created pressure (stress) from one's peers to do something you don't want to do. They make it so uncomfortable not to go along that the person agrees in order to relieve the pressure. Participation in something undesired increases because the stress of not going along becomes greater than the stress of agreeing to participate. Our guidance helps us avoid such situations and also lessens our reliance on the opinions of others for healthy self-esteem. Emotional Guidance will let you know the right decision. Your guidance knows it is not your job to make others' happy and it knows your goals and your agreements with yourself. If you don't want to do the thing you're being pressured to do, your guidance will help you find a way that is best for you. But it will go one step further. Your guidance seems to have foresight and if you train yourself to be sensitive to it, it can actually help you avoid being in the uncomfortable situation in the first place. You may be inspired to stay home on the night when the pressure would be uncomfortable or to accept an invitation from someone else for another activity or you may be inspired to go home at just the right time. I've spoken with individuals who, in hindsight, believe their guidance gave them an upset stomach that led to their leaving a situation they were later very happy to have escaped.

There are myriad examples of positive emotions seeming to lead to beneficial synchronicities. Researchers know negative life events are more likely during times of low emotional state, including accidents. Emotion can affect decisions about risk-taking in all age groups, not just adolescents'; the emotion doesn't necessarily have to be triggered by the situation itself. For example, a woman who is angry about an argument might drive too fast on the highway.[69]

Our emotions provide guidance, but for a very long time we have been teaching children (who are born knowing how to be joyful) to pay attention to pleasing others instead of following their natural guidance. Parents, teachers, ministers, and peers say, "Do this so I will feel better," and because the pressure is intense, children eventually begin using others as their barometer about how to behave. This is very problematic if you are trying to please more than one other person and even more problematic if one of those people is inconsistent about what pleases him.

Society has developed a belief that without external guidance our behavior would be unacceptable. Recent findings in positive psychology refute this premise. When individuals are in a positive state, they exhibit not only behaviors that society requires as *socially acceptable* but behaviors that go far beyond the minimums. Altruism and cooperation increase substantially when higher levels of positive emotion are present.

Helping children understand that listening to their own Emotional Guidance is important will change our world. We often speak of animals having instincts and humans having intellect. We do have instincts but we are trained not to listen to them. We all have guidance and we can hear it when we quiet our minds. What most do not do is listen to it or understand how it communicates. Our minds are powerful and important, but our hearts are even more intelligent. The HeartMath Institute conducted a study that showed the heart registered responses in a predictive manner, while the brain responded after the fact to the same stimuli.[70]

Retribution

Researchers have theorized that people's natural response to crime is a desire for retribution, "We suggest that the desire for retribution is people's initial, intuitive response to crimes."[71] I disagree. It appears intuitive only because almost everyone is trained from a young age to believe punishment is the proper response to wrongdoing. It is automatic in most adults because of the training—not a natural *inborn trait*. There is a consistent message, in the way misbehavior is dealt with that creates an, "I was punished so others should be as well." sense of fair play. This will never end without conscious decisions to end it. I was punished as a child. I knew the belt from my father and fists from my brother. But I understand that continuing that cycle improves nothing. I want a better world—not a fair world if a fair world requires an eye for an eye or continuation of practices that are not in humanity's best interests. A fair world might demand that all be equal—but all do not want the same. Whether a child is made to sit in the corner or spanked for transgressions, a belief develops that punishment is the appropriate response to misbehavior. Once a belief is developed it can appear to be an intuitive response, but that does not make it so.

Intuitive indicates from broader perspective—from God's viewpoint. Broader perspective sees it differently. I believe that any retribution in Holy Scriptures reflects, not a punishing God, but man's misinterpretation of God's messages through an interpreter who believed in retribution. Retribution and love are not the same vibration. When I go inward, I see the truth of "God is Love." (John 4:8) Love and retribution cannot abide in the same vibration.

The argument that the punishment is for the child's own good does not stand up to the known facts today. Punishing a child decreases the child's immune, cognitive, digestive and central nervous system functions if it decreases the child's emotional state. Punishment usually decreases mood, which also means that the likelihood of undesired behavior increases as the result of punishment (based on scientific research from many different studies). I, along with millions of other children, was *punished for my own good*. It was a prevalent belief during my childhood. It was based on false premises that had been passed on from generation to generation. We know more today. It is up to us to stop this unproductive cycle.

As with many aspects of scriptures, I can see how some men could benefit from creating fear of retribution. God, however, knows the true hearts of man and knows that fear negatively impacts behavior while love improves behavior. God would not want to strike fear in the hearts of mankind. Men who do not know their own power would.

Someone who has attuned himself so that he is consciously aware of his guidance in its more subtle forms knows his own power. Some would call it enlightened. It is not a state like a college degree that, once earned, is yours forevermore. It requires maintenance but with practice, it can become a habitual state. It is a state of Being in which one is consistently on the high end of the EGSc. Such a person demonstrates considerably equanimity even during situations that others find highly stressful.

Being the moral authority confers power. Someone who does not understand the power that is their birthright could seek power by creating fear. Mary Baker Eddy said it this way, "That God's wrath should be vented upon His beloved son, is divinely unnatural. Such a theory is man-made." [72, 73] and "Rabbi and priest taught the Mosaic law, which said: 'An eye for an eye,' and 'Whoso sheddeth man's blood, by man shall his blood be shed.' Not so did Jesus, the new executor for God, present the divine law of Love, which blesses even those that curse it."[74]

As far as the rightness of retribution, I have to consider that there is a vibrational match between victims and perpetrators. No one wants to hear this and discussions often end prematurely with claims that this is blaming the victim. I reject that perspective about such discussions because if the victim is doing something that attracts crime (and research clearly shows this is true) then understanding what that is and educating the public so they can consciously not do the thing that attracts perpetrators to them is a worthwhile endeavor. Unknowingly attracting a perpetuator does not mean the victim deserves what happens to him or her. It merely means that the crime is not nearly as random as most individuals seem to believe it is and I am not just referring to areas where poverty currently prevails.

Research on victim selection,[75] points to an unconscious factor that leads multiple convicted criminals to select the same individual as their target from videos. The factor is not yet fully understood by researchers. Psychological profiles of the victims indicate a victim mindset. The Metaphysician knows that a victim mindset indicates a victim vibration. The individual selected does not always appear, on the physical level, to be the weakest or easiest target. Once a woman has been raped, statistically her chances of being raped again increase[76] to seven times her risk of the first rape. Women who were sexually abused as children have a far greater risk of being raped after age 14 than those who were not abused as children.[77] The percentages vary by study (and the populations being studied) but the difference is vast in every study. One study showed over 68% of women who had been victims as children were victims of rape or attempted rape after age 14 compared to 38% of women with no childhood abuse history.[78] Another study, with much lower overall reported rates of rape and attempted rape, showed 26% of women with a history of childhood abuse were sexually assaulted as adults versus 3% of women with no history of childhood abuse.[79] The actual percentages are not as important[b] as the fact that a history of abuse creates a significantly increased risk of further victimization.

The underlying victim vibration attracts those who are seeking victims.

I know the difference between the underlying emotional stances and thoughts that underlie my personal experiences of repeated sexual victimization and how my experiences changed as I changed my thoughts. After the first rape, my level of fear was palpable. I am confident I was exuding, "I am a victim" in my vibration. The world responded to this vibration and brought me evidence to let me know how I was vibrating in additional experiences. I continued to attract those who were seeking victims until I changed my thoughts and vibration to that of a more empowered Being. I am no longer a match to these types of situations. The way the world responds to me changed as I changed my thoughts.

Understanding Emotional Guidance would help victims not vibrate exude victimhood and would help the potential criminal lower stress and improve mood, decreasing the likelihood he or she would commit a crime. I can also see how someone who has a vibration that is not serving her could become more and more desperate to feel more empowered—a desire that could ultimately lead to criminal behavior. That may be what happened when Stacey Lannert killed her father.

It feels counter-intuitive to help criminals feel better, but only because we have developed a belief that the proper response to undesired behavior is punishment. Gang research shows disturbing information that, if it were fully understood by the public, would show how irrational it is to punish someone who commits even violent crimes. The criminals are victims as much as their victims are victims.

A survey of 4,664 men from lower socioeconomic and high minority residents[80] revealed the following statistics for gang members:

- ➤ 85.8% had an antisocial personality disorder
- ➤ 66.6% were alcoholics
- ➤ 25.1% screened positive for psychosis
- ➤ 57.4% were drug dependent
- ➤ 34.2% had attempted suicide
- ➤ 58.9% had an anxiety disorder

---

[b] They are not as important for the purposes of this paper. For other purposes they are, of course, important. The variance has a great deal to do with the population being studied as some populations have a greater overall risk of sexual assault as do some lifestyle choices. Those are not topics being discussed in this paper.

I believe anyone who views this type of background information would perceive this population as needing help. Some might attribute their gang involvement with their illnesses, dependencies, and suicide attempts, but the far more likely scenario is that they were already stressed and feeling disconnected from others. The same study indicated that gang members had themselves been victims of violence, had high levels of fear about further victimization, and many suffer from PTSD.

The most common scenario that I see is a series of circumstances where life seems to punish an individual that results in low emotional states which leads to retaliation through crime, or to drugs and alcohol use, which then leads to crime. The research shows a clear correlation between life skills and lower crime rates, even in adverse circumstances.

Protective factors reduce the negative impact of multiple stressors on child development. Increasing protective factors lessens the negative impacts of poverty and other childhood stressors. The combination of both family and neighborhood stressors had the highest negative effect and contributed to current and future aggression in both boys and girls. "The core assertion of this theory (General Strain Theory) is that the presence of strains in the life of an individual can lead to feelings of fear, depression, anger, and frustration. Such negative emotions can generate pressure for corrective action, resulting in risky behaviours that may be deviant or criminal, including internalising behaviors such as substance misuse, and externalising behaviours such as violence and theft"[81]

Stressful life events are associated with higher aggression in children. "Positive emotions are not mere epiphenomena. They broaden thought and action repertoires, increase mental flexibility, augment meaning-based coping, and motivate engagement in novel activities and social relationships. Importantly, positive emotions, although transient, have lasting consequences; they build durable personal resources whose accrual triggers further positive emotions, leading to self-sustaining upward spirals of well-being.

Conversely, when negative emotions accrete into downward spirals of defensive behavior, focus on threat, and feelings of inefficacy, these self-destructive, vicious cycles can lead to impoverished life experiences, and potentially, devastating psychopathology. The structural differences between upward and downward spirals are largely incompatible, and thus positive emotions may exert a countervailing force on the dysphoric, fearful, and anhedonic states characteristic of persons with emotion-related disorders. Hence, upward spirals can counter downward spirals."[82, 83] I disagree with the researchers insofar as the transitory nature of positive emotions. The researchers are not using Emotional Guidance, which can be used to develop habits of thought that maintain positive emotional stances. Beyond that, the impact of emotion on outcome is clear.

When we understand that higher emotional states equate to more desirable behaviors, we will understand the importance of fostering higher emotional states in ourselves and others. Punishments tend to keep people at low emotional states and progress is very slow, if it happens at all. Helping someone with undesirable behavior feel better goes against what almost everyone has been taught from a young age. On the other hand, when we look at how things really unfold, we understand that this is the only path to permanent improvement and perhaps even, eradication of many socially unacceptable behaviors (in time when this is understood and commonly practiced by societies).

What do we really want: to punish criminals or to prevent individuals from becoming criminals in the first place? Right now, the resources flow to punishing criminals and attempts to prevent crime although the law is clear that no individual has the right to assert that law enforcement should have prevented them from being a victim of any given crime. Law enforcement is a deterrent by their presence in theory, but they cannot prevent specific crimes.

There is a plethora of growing evidence suggesting that social ills including crime, teen pregnancy, drug and alcohol abuse, and more are casually related to long-term emotional pain. There is also mounting evidence that indicates improved desirable behaviors are linked to increased positive emotion including better corporate citizenship, altruism, kindness to strangers without expectation of reward, better relationships of all types, and much more, "At the interpersonal level… positive emotions increase people's sense of 'oneness' with close others."[84, 85] Peil suggests the true nature of humans: we are all good at our core.[86] Seligman echoes this argument in *Flourish*[87] and Dacher Keltner reinforces it in *Born to be Good*.[88] However, only when Emotional Guidance is followed consistently is our true nature demonstrated. Prolonged negative emotions that result when Emotional Guidance is ignored often lead to undesirable behaviors.

Labels

Humans label others by characteristics, behavior, and appearance. We then apply judgments based on the labels we assign to others and ourselves. Labels save time and help us navigate life, but they can also greatly diminish outcomes. Labels distort our perspective in every area. Even labels about colors have been shown to distort our perception based on research that demonstrates that different regions of the world label the same color differently.[89, 90]

Individual behavior varies largely due to the current emotional state of the individual. When we judge based on behavior without an understanding of the impact of emotional state, individuals at lower emotional states tend to be judged harshly and their potential greatly underestimated. For example, the same individual feeling despair would not respond to a situation the way he or she would when happy. For the observer, who is also an influencer in many situations, the solution is to perceive others based on their potential, not their current behavior.

For the individual, the solution is to decide for oneself who you are. Emotional Guidance will support a positive self-image with positive emotions in response to positive thoughts about self. Once trust in one's Emotional Guidance has been developed, the positive response facilitates developing healthy self-worth. It can also help reduce the dependence of self-esteem on specific groups that can make maintaining healthy self-esteem more difficult.

Labels can be detrimental to the person who has negatively labeled other groups of people. When we label a group as bad, *evil*, or inferior, we feel negative emotion when we think of that group. Most people interpret this emotion as reinforcing their negative view. Every time they think of that group of people they feel bad. They believe that means the group they are thinking about has a flaw. But the real reason they feel bad is because their *higher self* disagrees with their negative view about the group, no matter how justified the negative label may be.

Don't take my word for it. If you have labeled a group as bad in some way, try softening your beliefs about the group and see if your emotional response does not feel better. Let's take a gang known for violence. If you've labeled them as bad, perhaps railing against them verbally when the news reports more of their violence, see how you feel if you shift your thoughts. Try telling yourself that they are doing the best they can given the environment they are in and knowledge they currently possess. Try telling yourself that if they had different skills their behavior would improve—that they are not inherently bad. Try considering that they simply lack productive skills and are doing their best to survive.

You don't have to shift your opinion a lot to feel enough of an emotional difference to know it feels better. You can't leap from seeing a group as horrible to good in one leap. But you can move in the direction of feeling better one step at a time.

Your negative labels about others harms you by causing you negative emotion, which decreases your immune, cognitive, digestive and central nervous system function. It is not their behavior; it's your perception about their behavior that makes you feel as awful as you do. From that negative emotional state you don't have cognitive access to solutions. When you shift your thoughts to seeing the group members as doing their best under the circumstances, you leave room for solutions that can create space for them to do better.

I often encounter individuals who have broad negative beliefs about one or more groups, but have personal relationships that are contrary to those broad beliefs. There is an obvious disconnect between what they have been taught to believe and their actual experience. I met one man who was very anti-sematic on a broad, general level yet his best friend was Jewish. This was indicative of someone who has accepted beliefs others taught him without question. It would be very easy for someone like this to use his Emotional Guidance to overthrow the anti-Semitism that is not serving him.

I've known other people who had racially or religiously based prejudices who had friends from the group they were prejudice against. They would argue that their friend was an exception, but if there is one exception to the rule, it's not a rule. Again, emotional guidance can help overthrow prejudices we were taught and adopted without question.

Mental and Physical Abuse: Chain Reactions

That abused children are far more likely to become violent themselves is a well-documented and accepted fact in scientific circles termed *the cycle of violence.*[91, 92, 93, 94, 95, 96, 97, 98, 99, 100, and 101]

In addition to a greatly increased risk of being on the wrong side of law enforcement, adults who were abused as children have, on average, far worse outcomes in health and lifestyle than adults who were not abused. This includes increased drug and alcohol dependence, increased likelihood of being a sex worker, PTSD, tobacco use, medical problems and overall poor quality of life.[102, 103, 104, 105, 106, and 107] Early intervention and treatment improves outcomes.[108]

Generally, studies have found a graded relationship between the cumulative number of adverse event exposures and adult health-risk behaviors and diseases.[109]

My stance is that teaching children coping skills is the solution. We have attempted to stop the abuse through criminalization for decades without success. The solution is to stop the *cycle of violence* by providing victims with knowledge of their Emotional Guidance System that enables them to achieve self-mastery of their emotional stance thus increasing emotional intelligence, resilience, and coping skills that reduce aggression.[110] The American Psychological Association provides the following teaching tip regarding self-efficacy.

"Self-efficacy refers to an individual's belief in his or her capacity to execute behaviors necessary to produce specific performance attainments (Bandura, 1977, 1986, 1997). Self-efficacy reflects confidence in the ability to exert control over one's own motivation, behavior, and social environment. These cognitive self-evaluations influence all manner of human experience, including the goals for which people strive, the amount of energy expended toward goal achievement, and likelihood of attaining particular levels of behavioral performance. Unlike traditional psychological constructs, self-efficacy beliefs are hypothesized to vary depending on the domain of functioning and circumstances surrounding the occurrence of behavior."[111]

Properly used, Emotional Guidance can improve the cognitive self-evaluations in any situation.

Research clearly demonstrates that the outcome can be improved via "…efficient self-regulation, active coping styles, optimism, and secure attachment were observed in youth who had faced adverse situations and settings, yet did not succumb to the adverse impact of extreme stress."[112] Using one's Emotional Guidance is an active coping style that leads to efficient self-regulation, optimism and supports forming secure attachments by reinforcing positive perspectives about those with whom one has relationships. Emotional Guidance exists to provide us with a way to navigate life and cope well with adversity.

Taking the stance that the abuser is also a victim goes against the grain and strongly held beliefs held by most of society. One reason is the idea that someone pushed beyond certain limits can become a *bad* person creates the fear that we could become that *bad* person. Believing *badness* is a trait provides us some emotional security that we would not become that person. This stance, while it feels better to anyone who does not have the skills to master their own emotional stance, provides a false sense of security.

What if law enforcement officers understood that to deter crime, potential criminals had to learn how to feel more empowered in a healthy way? The truth is that many of us would be capable of atrocities if we shared the history of those who commit them. It is the difference in our experiences, or our response to our experiences, not a difference in our innate *goodness* that separates us.

Not all individuals who suffer abuse become abusers. Their saving grace is the mental processes they use to cope with adversity and to make sense of their world. One wrong conclusion can lead to another and another. Our society fails miserably at teaching our children about the results of flawed thinking. We tell them not to do things and even not to think things, but we do not teach them how to think positively. A child who understood his or her Emotional Guidance would understand their thinking was flawed when they made the first wrong conclusion, which would prompt them to re-evaluate and change their conclusion.

Even a child who has developed a worldview based on a series of wrong conclusions can become stable on a better path rather quickly once they learn about their Emotional Guidance and the connection between Emotional State and Behavior. The most frequent question I have when I work in schools after the children learn about how Emotional State affects perception is whether it is possible that one of their parents has been angry their entire life. The relief on their faces when they learn that yes, someone who has developed angry patterns of thought can (and will) have a chronically angry emotional state is easy to read.

Children want to please their parents. A chronically angry parent is not pleasable. Most children will decide that there is something wrong with themselves when their efforts to please a parent repeatedly fail. Learning that it is the parents' chronic emotional state and not some inherent flaw in themselves that has made them unable to please a parent is a huge relief. Most of them feel compassion for the parent and relief about not being flawed just because they have not been able to please the parent.

Other times, children are not able to please a parent because the parent rigidly wants to define who they should be based on the parent's values. The child in this situation has two choices. The first is attempting to live according to the dictates of the parent and not being true to his or her self. This usually does not turn out well in the long run. I'm not talking about whether the child obeys parental rules about safety, sleep, homework, and other areas of conflict. I'm referring to a parent who values sports not being supportive of his studious son, or the businessman who does not want his son to follow his dreams of a musical career and to the mother who wants her daughter to marry a nice boy and start a family when the daughter wants to wait for a romance that sweeps her off her feet.

One kind person whose words provide hope can change the future path of an abused child. One disparaging remark from an influential individual can have a tremendous impact—positive or negative depending on the interpretation. Acceptance of the unkind words as the truth makes things worse; many a child has been saved by adopting an "I'll show you" attitude that rejects the unkind definition of self. I've had several clients who joined the military to *prove* to a demanding parent that they had value. I don't understand the concept because in my worldview everyone has tremendous value. It is not up to anyone else to judge the value of another or their potential. I have a long list of individuals that were, at one time, considered failures who are well-known successful people today. One example is Eckhart Tolle who spent a number of years being homeless before writing a book that sold over 3 million copies.

I also know that the expectations we have about others frequently influences the outcomes they achieve. In *Our Children Live in a War Zone,* considerable attention is devoted to this subject and how we can best manage it to help our family, students, peers and even strangers thrive. A child who learns how to use Emotional Guidance can negate verbal abuse even when it comes from a parent.

Providing information about our Emotional Guidance system and how to accurately interpret its messages builds skills with great flexibility to adjust to changing and unique circumstances. "Other studies have found that neural circuits involved in resilience can be modified for many years after adversity. For instance, the majority of adolescents whose development was stunted in childhood due to trauma were able to developmentally 'catch-up' when relocated to a supportive, loving environment."[113, 114]

With all that I am, I believe goodness resides in the heart of everyone. Given a path that allows one to simultaneously feel better (more empowered) and be nicer, I believe it will always be chosen over a path that provides the same feeling of empowerment but requires one to be less kind. Only those who do not understand the kinder path is open to them will choose the one that is more harmful to self and others.

What we've been trying (criminalization) has not worked. The problem worsens on a daily basis. We have created a society with a deep, dark underbelly. It is time to move in a new direction. This is not a call to stop the current methods, but to add to them. Teach children (all children—because we have no real idea who is suffering abuse), self-mastery and about their Emotional Guidance System. The results will point the way for the future—a vastly improved future.

As many adults as possible should also be taught, with an emphasis on parents, teachers, criminal justice and social workers, incarcerated and paroled individuls, and business leaders who can introduce the concepts to their employee base. Public service educational announcements and television shows or webcasts are other ways this information can quickly and affordably be communicated.

Effective Training Works

Problem-solving and emotional intelligence training is effective in decreasing aggression.[115] I have seen transformative changes that many did not believe were possible. I have seen older individuals release long-held anger and resentment. I have seen adolescents so full of anger they barely functioned in normal environments let go of the anger and increase their resilience and self-sufficiency as a result.

Most people's lives are not what they would like them to be. Some people are satisfied in some areas but not others. Some people are unsatisfied with every area of their life. The details of their life have little bearing on how they feel. There are people living lives I would never want that are relatively satisfied and others living lives of luxury that are very dissatisfied.

Mastering our perceptions and enjoying the journey leads to greater life satisfaction and, ultimately, greater accomplishment.

One might ask why these ideas have not been implemented previously. The study of psychology focused almost exclusively on "…this pathology approach (which) has, besides its assets, also a serious liability, and that is an exaggerated emphasis on the morbid manifestations and on the lower aspects of human nature and the consequent unwarranted generalized applications of the many findings of psychopathology to the psychology of normal human beings. This has produced a rather dreary and pessimistic picture of human nature and the tendency to consider its higher values and achievements as derived only from the lower drives, through processes of reaction formation, transformation, and sublimation. Moreover, many important realities and functions have been neglected or ignored: intuition, creativity, the will, and the very core of the human psyche—the Self."[116, 117]

Also, the truth is that all the old masters knew what I am sharing in this book. But humanity plays small. We assume that people like Plato, Aristotle, Michelangelo, Socrates, Napoleon Hill, and all the great religious leaders, Martin Luther King, Jr., Mahatma Gandhi, Einstein, Michael Jordan, Oprah, and Mother Teresa are somehow different from us. It's one reason we can become so upset and disillusioned when we learn they had failings. They were human, just like us. They had good days and bad days, just like us. They were no better than our potential. They simply manifested more of their potential than *ordinary people* typically do.

There is nothing standing between *ordinary people* and greatness other than their own mindset. By putting the Great Ones on a pedestal, we tell the filters in our mind that they are different from us—that we are not one of the Great Ones. That is the same as telling our filter we cannot be a Great One. It does not serve us. I'm not talking about having a huge ego. I'm not talking about seeing ourself as better than others. I shared the perfect way to perceive ourself and others in the Humility chapter. We have to believe ourselves capable of something before we are capable of it.

Humans have an amazing capacity for unexpected greatness. Every time there is a disaster the stories of ordinary hero's come to the surface. We are all greater than we pretend to be. We have to give ourselves permission to be all we can be—to not play small.

In *A Return to Love: Reflections on the Principles of "A Couse in Miracles"* Marianne Williamson wrote:

"Our deepest fear is not that we are inadequate. Our deepest fear is that we are powerful beyond measure. It is our light, not our darkness that most frightens us. We ask ourselves, 'Who am I to be brilliant, gorgeous, talented, and fabulous?' Actually, who are you not to be? You are a child of God. Your playing small does not serve the world. There is nothing enlightened about shrinking so that other people won't feel insecure around you. We are all meant to shine, as children do. We were born to make manifest the glory of God that is within us. It's not just in some of us; it's in everyone. And as we let our own light shine, we unconsciously give other people permission to do the same. As we are liberated from our own fear, our presence automatically liberates others."

I think she nailed it. By playing small we deprive the world of our gifts. I was a successful Executive when all the pieces of the puzzle finally clicked into place. I had a comfortable, low-risk life. I was enjoying international travel and a beautiful home in a golf course community. I could have played small. I could have just used this knowledge for my own benefit. I did not have to learn how to communicate the information in a bunch of different ways so individuals with widely different worldviews could and would use it. I did not have to leave my safe career and venture in the world of entrepreneurship, publishing, and speaking outside my traditional career. I did not have to write a dozen books in five years, presenting the root cause solution to society's social ills in a variety of ways. I could have played small and safe.

By not playing small I've changed a lot of lives and am poised to improve even more. As a speaker, I often do not know how much difference I make in the lives of people I speak to, but I know I've prevented more than one suicide and inspired changes that made significant improvements in many lives. I would not give any of it up. I know at least one of the people I helped was on a trajectory that is very similar to the ones we hear about when the news focuses on the perpetrators of heinous crimes and that understanding his guidance took him off that path. Would he have been a news headline someday that brought the country's flags to half-mast? I can't say he would have been, but I can say he won't be.

I'm not bragging about what I've done. I'm showing you the power of the words in this book. I'm showing you that ordinary people can do extraordinary things. I don't think I'm any different than anyone else—I just know a lot more about this subject than most do because I have been thinking about human thriving for over two decades. The more you step into the path of living larger, the more possibilities open up for you.

My work has focused almost exclusively on what makes humans thrive—the opposite of morbid pathology. The chronic stress pathway to undesired behaviors that increase the likelihood of criminal activity has been demonstrated repeatedly. The protective aspects of learning good stress management have also been demonstrated repeatedly.

It is important to model positive behavior and emotional states using emotional guidance, but modeling alone is not sufficient. This knowledge has been with us throughout recorded history, albeit without as much support from so many disciplines. People model many wonderful behaviors and most people think, "I couldn't do that or be like that." They don't know how to go from where they are (truthfully, where society trained them to be) to the kinder, gentler, happier person they were born to be. It is possible for anyone to learn, but they need step-by-step instructions or a lighted path and encouragement that they are good enough and that they can be that good. Historically, individuals who achieved this state were put on pedestals, separating them from the average person and increasing the belief that only special people could achieve such states.

Let's Roll

In the first century A.D., Seneca exhorted his fellow Greeks, "He who does not prevent a crime when he can, encourages it," and Cicero added, "Every evil in the bud is easily crushed." Since Seneca and Cicero, the cloak of prevention has been wrapped around a large body of interventions.[118]

When Emotional Guidance is correctly interpreted, it will guide each person to personal satisfaction and happiness which brings us right around to reducing crime.

The concept of an *evil* person was developed to protect us from the fear that we could behave in the abhorrent ways we sometimes observe in others. If some people are *good* and some are *evil*, we are not at risk of being one of the *evil* ones if we follow the rules that make us *good*. Although I believe the concept has been perpetuated by authorities who gained power by being the authoritative source for determining what was *good* and what was *evil*, it is not fruitful to delve deeply into that aspect of the topic. It is enough to help the world understand that no one is inherently *evil*.

The reduction of fear will increase the flow of ideas. "…many positive emotions broaden individuals' momentary thought-action repertoires, prompting them to pursue a wider range of thoughts and actions than is typical."[119] Companies will benefit from the greater cognitive skills in their employees, which will lead to new innovation.[120]

 Health care expenses and absenteeism will decrease as the physical and mental benefits of increased positivity and optimism are experienced. Turnover will decrease and productivity will rise. Employee engagement will rise.

From the broader perspective, the world will move closer to achieving peace. Understanding our Emotional Guidance system and incorporating it into our lives, including our social and corporate structures, is the key to changes so many desire. For the first time in recorded history the pieces of the puzzle are understood and the means to achieve them are available to everyone.

For many years it is has been common for people to encourage one another to *Think Positive*, but now, for the first time, the question of *How* to think more positively is available. Individuals can shift from wherever they are—whether they are chronically depressed or mildly happy—to greater thriving.

The root cause of that empty feeling that many otherwise successful people struggle to fill can be satisfied, enabling them to feel a greater sense of wholeness.

In *The Happiness Hypothesis*, Jonathan Haidt describes "The myth of pure evil is the ultimate self-serving bias, the ultimate form of naïve realism."[121] He speaks of it as a way to protect the ego. While it may have begun in this way, it was perpetuated by religious teachings from many worldviews and I believe this was motivated by a desire to control others' actions and, sometimes, to provide a rallying cry that motivated followers to fight for a common cause. Of course, it is a chicken and egg sort of thing; at this point there is no way to know which came first.

I base my assertion that punishment is not ethical on the basis that behavior is better when a person feels good and worse when a person feels bad. Punishment is designed to make an individual feel worse, which ensures the continuation or escalation of undesired behavior. There are instances when punishment makes an individual feel better, but those situations do not negate the fact that the design of the punishment was to make the person feel bad about their behavior.

In the same way that illnesses such as cancer and heart disease are considered something bad that happens to the body of an individual, the inclination and willingness to harm others—physically, emotionally, or spiritually—can also be seen to be a form of illness—something other than a healthy, thriving human. Humans, in their optimum state, are good to one another. Any departure from that is an illness—of the mind, body, or spirit. We would not seek to punish individuals who develop physical illnesses like cancer and heart disease. Punishment of those who harm others is no more a cure than it would be to punish someone who has become ill with something we recognize and acknowledge as an illness.

The entire concept of crime as something other than illness is because of the classification system and labels mankind has applied to it. These labels were applied in the past when we did not have a clear understanding of the fact that a thriving human treats others well. The mistaken thinking that some people are inherently *good* and others are inherently *evil* brought humanity to this erroneous conclusion and it is time to reject that premise in light of overwhelming scientific evidence demonstrating that humans who are happy treat others well.

Illness, whether it is in the form of a recognized medical problem or in the form of recognized crimes, is a departure from our optimal nature and wellbeing. The root cause is the same in all cases.

Someone who has been feeling guilty may feel better (due to a sense of relief) when they come clean about a transgression and accept a punishment they believe is just for what they have done. This is one of the rare situations where the person feels better as a result of punishment. However, **the reason** the rare person feels better is not because they are punished. The **reason is** the self-punishment (usually in self-denigrating thoughts) the person has been inflicting on himself is worse than the punishment society prescribes, which allows him to give himself permission to cease the self-torture. It must be noted that this individual, already feeling remorse and guilt or even shame for his actions, was not likely to repeat the behavior even if he was not punished by society. If the person was not doing something to himself that made the punishment society proscribed feel better than what he was doing to himself because of the transgression, he would not feel better when coming clean and paying society's price.

We were designed by our Creator to function at our best when we feel good. Our functioning in all areas, not just behavior, declines as our emotional state declines. I believe our emotions are guidance from Source designed to show us our path of least resistance toward our highest potential. When we are moving toward that potential, we feel great. The degree to which we are moving in opposition to our highest potential determines how bad we feel.

Our path of least resistance requires some clarification. While the path of least resistance toward our desire is a straight line, *our path* may not be a straight line. Source can see the path but Source also knows what we are likely to hear and understand from our guidance. The filters in our minds make a straight path unlikely unless we have practiced listening clearly. I'll give you an example. I wanted to find a book. We have bookcases in every room in our home and there is no clear organization. I'd already looked in the areas I thought the specific book I wanted would be without success. Then I felt inspired to tend to a task in our dining room—a place where a small bookcase has been stashed due to lack of room elsewhere. The task I was inspired to tend to was not something urgent. It has been on my list for weeks. As I began the task I dropped something, bent over to pick it up, and with my eyes now level with the lowest shelf of the bookcase in the dining room, I spotted the book I had been seeking. It was under another, larger book. The only way I would have found it was by being eye level with the lowest shelf.

Many will find this example extremely far-fetched, but if they ask themselves if believing it is possible will harm them in any way, I believe the answer will be no. If you want to test this in your own life, it is easy to look for and find evidence of synchronicities that happen all the time. They are so frequent and common that we take them for granted, but when taken apart and dissected as I did with the example above, someone open to the possibility of subtle guidance helping them day-in and day-out takes on a life of its own.

When we look for evidence of this, it is prevalent. We are inspired to do and say things that help us in big and small ways. Another example is that I love to uplift people. Sometimes when I am out and about I am inspired to say something to complete strangers that, the old me who did not understand my guidance and who was too concerned about what others might think, would have never said I follow that inspiration. The most common response to my comment is, "Oh, thank you. That is exactly what I needed to hear right now."

Often it is a simple word of encouragement to a harried Mom in line at a store. Other times it is someone who is alone whose presence offers few clues about what words might be beneficial at that time yet the appreciation in the response is just as enthusiastic. It's not just polite appreciation. It's more than that. It is truly what the person needed at that exact moment. I'm just not smart enough to figure this stuff out on my own. It is coming from Source and I am a willing participant.

Our path of least resistance considers our beliefs. If I do not believe the straight line is possible my guidance will encourage me to take another path toward my goals. It won't be the shortest path, but it is the shortest path I can take with my current beliefs. The more we pay attention to the subtlest guidance, the clearer the presence of guidance becomes. Just a few days spent being mindful of synchronicities demonstrates how present and valuable guidance is in our lives.

The Urantia Book says, "Fear and shame are unworthy motivations for religious living. Religion is valid only when it reveals the fatherhood of God and enhances the brotherhood of men."[122]

Emotional Guidance creates more positive emotions. The effect is self-sustaining because there are intrinsic rewards for using Emotional Guidance that are felt immediately and increase over time. Although the following comment pertains to a work environment, researchers have found that positivity is reinforced by the benefits it confers and, "...also support the notion that positivity is potentially self-sustainable as the employees positive experiences generate a desire for maintaining and sustaining positive workplace climate, which establishes an on-going cycle of reproduction of positive workplace perceptions, emotions and behaviors that eventually become incorporated and internalized in the workplace environment."[123] The benefits of positivity may be greater outside work, because of the personal importance attributed to our primary relationships, which should increase its self-sustainability.

I cannot speak to whether we can cure all current criminals by teaching them these methods; I do believe the attempt would be a worthwhile endeavor. However, I believe with all that I am that we can come close to eliminating future criminals by teaching Emotional Guidance to the world's children and, to the extent possible, to their parents, teachers, and other adults.

Science has clearly demonstrated that happy individuals do not commit crimes, yet our current system strives to make those who commit crimes feel worse—something we know will lead to continuing and increased criminal activity. It is clear that the current system is not working and is on a trajectory where it will eventually fall under its own weight. There were 14 million arrests in 2010.[124]

Both science and religion point to Emotional Guidance as a way of knowing the shortest possible path to each individual's unique highest good. The skills necessary to develop a high level of sustainable happiness using Emotional Guidance and other simple and easy to learn skills that increase True Happiness can be inexpensively taught to large groups and understood by young children. The benefit of teaching these skills on a widespread basis more than offsets the cost when it is compared to the price society currently bears for incarceration and trials. Even without giving consideration to the relief of pain and suffering by criminals, victims, and their families it makes sense to implement a widespread program from both a humanitarian and cost perspective, not to mention social justice.

Although not discussed in this book, other proven benefits of increased positivity are enormous including significant improvements in health,[125, 126, 127, 128, 129] productivity,[130] relationships,[131] and more.

It is time for brave individuals to step up and point out that the current system is fatally flawed. It is not achieving society's desires. In fact, it is not achieving the purpose for which societies were formed—making living together safer than living outside society. Reforms will not fix the problem. We have to be smart enough and bold enough to look at the situation in an entirely new way, apply cutting edge science to the problem of crime, and then move forward with a solution that solves the problem at its root.

Many in the system will defend it, in part because they do not want to acknowledge they've participated in something so broken. But they need to accept that they were doing the best they could, that their intentions were good and they were taught false premises that almost everyone has believed were true for a long time. It is only recently that science is showing the fallacy at the root of the idea that making someone feel worse will improve his or her behavior. It is time for a paradigm shift. I would encourage individuals who have supported the old system to consider teaching the children about their guidance and simple skills that reduce stress and increase happiness. The benefits to areas other than reduction of crime are enormous and make a compelling case independent of this one for providing every child and as many adults as possible with these skills and knowledge. "Findings suggest that positive psychological well-being consistently protects against cardiovascular disease..."[132] Positivity decreases the risk of heart disease by 50%.[133] Heart disease is the world's number one cause of death. Positivity skills decrease the risk of depression and suicide even more. The cost to society of just these three things (heart disease, depression, and suicide) is estimated to be $758 Billion each year in the United States.[134, 135, and 136]

There is more than one way to look at the cost of incarceration. In 1999, David Anderson undertook the daunting task of estimating the total annual cost to society of crime by considering this general study considers all of the direct and indirect costs of crime in the United States. Anderson added the costs of crime to victims and prisoner's time, the cost of private deterrence and other factors that are not considered when only the cost to tax payers is analyzed. The results, published in the *Journal of Law and Economics*, was $1.7 Trillion dollars a year.[137] More recently, the *Statement of Principles* of the newly formed Law Enforcement Leaders To Reduce Crime & Incarceration indicated the direct cost of crime to taxpayers is 80 Billion each year in the United States.[138] There are approximately 321 million people in the United States.[139]

While reading Robert Assagioli's *Psychosynthesis*, I realized that the processes I recommend could be described in the same way he described Psychosynthesis:

"A method of psychological development and self-realization for those who refuse to remain the slaves of their own inner phantasms or of external influences, who refuse to submit passively to the play of psychological forces which is going on within them, and who are determined to become the master of their own lives."[140]

The current response to undesired behaviors is punishment of the individual who behaves inappropriately. Punishment for unacceptable behavior begins almost as soon as a toddler learns to walk and continues to be the predominant response to undesired behavior throughout life. This usual reaction to undesired behavior by parents, teachers, clergy, and other authority figures is done under the assumption that mankind is inherently bad, or sinful, and that without threat of punishment havoc would reign supreme. It is a stance that is based on a false premise that leads to the incarceration of greater percentages of humanity in each generation.

Punishment is seen as a deterrent, a way of preventing crime, and as a way of providing justice to victims and their families. It achieves neither. It is past time to apply science to crime prevention. Almost thirty years ago, Nietzel and Himelein suggested that developing cognitive, behavioral, academic, and occupational competencies would provide important buffers in youths' struggles to cope with stress and prevent them from becoming criminals.[141] Many have suffered unnecessarily because their recommendations were not implemented on a broad basis.

The criminal justice system is not working because it is rotten at its roots—the belief that man is sinful in nature and will behave poorly if the threat of punishment is not severe enough to control behavior

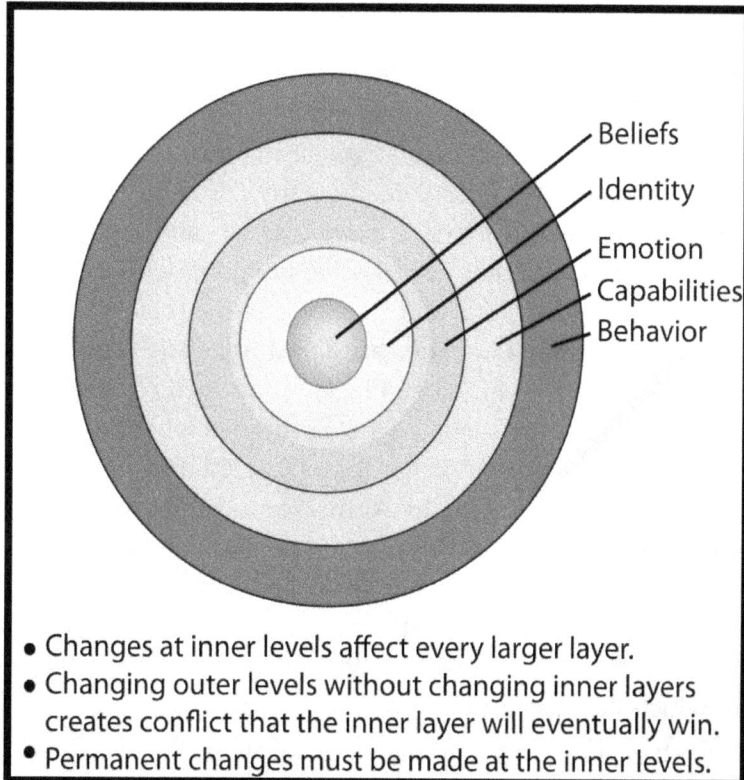

Beliefs
Identity
Emotion
Capabilities
Behavior

- Changes at inner levels affect every larger layer.
- Changing outer levels without changing inner layers creates conflict that the inner layer will eventually win.
- Permanent changes must be made at the inner levels.

is bogus. This is not working well for society as a whole or for the many millions whose lives are directly affected, whether as a victim, perpetrator, or families torn apart by the incarceration of a loved one.

Our beliefs create filters between our unconscious and conscious mind that are used to determine what information will be passed to the conscious mind because the unconscious processes millions of times more data that we become aware of. Our mind attempts to prove our beliefs to us and will go to great lengths to create back stories that explain the world in a way that is consistent with our beliefs. This filtering effect makes us interpret reality as if beliefs that are not true are reality.

Beliefs are at the root of our actions and even our thoughts. Beliefs affect every other area of life as shown in the diagram.

The solution requires a global change of perception about man's nature and a new approach to undesired behavior that has its roots in a clear understanding that humanity behaves in life promoting ways when individuals are happy and in life diminishing ways when individuals are unhappy. It also requires an understanding of the skills that lead to individual happiness including accurate interpretation of one's Emotional Guidance.

The global potential for improvement in lives and reduction of costs associated with crime is enormous. The burden of incarceration extends from the hard dollar costs to the effect on families torn apart and left destitute by the current system. It is not difficult to teach children skills that will increase their resilience, emotional intelligence, happiness, immune function, resistance to peer pressure, lower their stress levels, and lead to more pro-social behaviors. This includes significant reductions in the risk of addictions that so often lead to criminal behavior.

Jonathan Haidt, considered one of the top global thinkers by many, wrote in his doctoral dissertation, *Moral judgment, affect, and culture, or, is it wrong to eat your dog?* "In middle and late childhood, cognitive development has advanced to the point where the child understands the mental operation of reversibility, and its analog in the social domain, reciprocity. At this stage, children understand and care about rules and fairness, and they enjoy truly interactive social play. However, when Piaget questioned children about where rules come from, and how they can be changed, he discovered what he called a "heteronomous" orientation, in which rules are regarded as "sacred and untouchable, emanating from adults and lasting forever."[142] At this second stage, rules have an authority and an existence of their own, like laws of physics which are external to people and cannot be changed by consensus. Piaget calls this reification of social rules "moral realism," which he defines as "the tendency which the child has to regard duty and the value attaching to it as selfsubsistent and independent of the mind, as imposing itself regardless of the circumstances in which the individual may find himself."[143]

He goes on to say that the third stage allows for the change of the rules, "They should recognize that rules are made by societies for the mutual benefit of their members, and that these rules can be changed, especially if they do not protect people from harm.[144]

He continues by stating that authoritative parenting can delay the realization of this third stage and cites research demonstrating that the lower socio-economic classes tend to be more authoritative resulting in those "…who obey rules out of fear while milder discipline, coupled with explanations and 'induction' produces the greatest internalization"[145]

Going on to discuss Kohlberg who built upon Piaget's earlier work, the conventional level (stages 3 and 4) is described as having the characteristic "…maintaining the expectations of the individual's family, group, or nation is perceived as valuable in its own right, regardless of immediate and obvious consequences."[146] I believe this is why we continue using punishment in response to crime and are failing to recognize that the punishment is not effective and it does not deter crime—it also increases future crimes. Laws designed to protect us are, in fact, harming us but they continue because we do not consciously recognize that we are stuck in the conventional level of morality.

Haidt concludes with a description of a more evolved view of morality, "Post-conventional thinkers attempt to ground moral rules in first principles, and do not accept tradition or authority as a sufficient justification for condemning or punishing people. Almost all post-conventional thinking is carried out at stage 5, which takes as its first principles the rights and welfare of people. Rules which protect rights and maximize welfare will be endorsed. Rules which infringe upon rights without any strong benefit to welfare will be opposed."[147]

Should my goal be to develop post-conventional thinking on a widespread basis or to change the social norm, making vast beneficial changes to the system of crime and punishment possible without requiring society's level of cognitive thinking to increase? I believe it is both. The reason I believe this is that there are other issues—that contribute to crime and other social ills—that can be resolved with better thinking.

Haidt's work helped me to see that the herd mentality that leads young people raised in poverty to believe they have no way out is indicative of conventional thinking. The belief is treated as a rule that maintains the expectations of the group.

It is difficult for modern humans to accept that they have something more valuable than their brain to guide them through life—until they experiment with their Emotional Guidance. Using your own Emotional Guidance is the only way to really understand how it works and how valuable it is. Many students have said it feels as if they are cheating because life became so much easier and made so much more sense. Almost all of us are accustomed to some level of struggle—so familiar that we only notice it by its absence. Rich or poor, this tension exists when we ignore or misinterpret our guidance.

Guidance is not cheating. It is how it was meant to be. For many, the concept of their own life being easier becomes twisted as it moves through filters (biases) created by beliefs they have developed and feelings of unworthiness arise. Sometimes it is necessary to take an end run around it in order to find acceptance. If you find yourself struggling with this, think about what you want for others—especially the children. Of course you want their lives to be easier, for them to find the way to their greatest achievements without each day being a struggle with relationships or wealth and health, and with emotional well-being. Most people have an easier time seeing that their desire for others to have this is good and pure. Once you go there in your mind and see it clearly, turn it to yourself and ask "Then why not me?" Your mind may make up all sorts of reasons but if you use your Emotional Guidance to refute those reasons you can come to an acceptance that you are also worthy. Another way to speed up this process is to understand that your worth and value to others increases substantially when you are positively focused and happy.

Some programs teach people to lower goals in order to be satisfied with one's life. I believe this path flies in the face of human nature. We are designed to always seek improvement—no matter how wonderful something is—our minds automatically ask, "How could it be better?" This is because our *Higher* or *Ideal Self* is always more than we are—never less. We are called toward becoming more.

Stress and Happiness

Happiness and stress move in opposite directions. When happiness increases, stress declines. When stress increases, happiness declines.

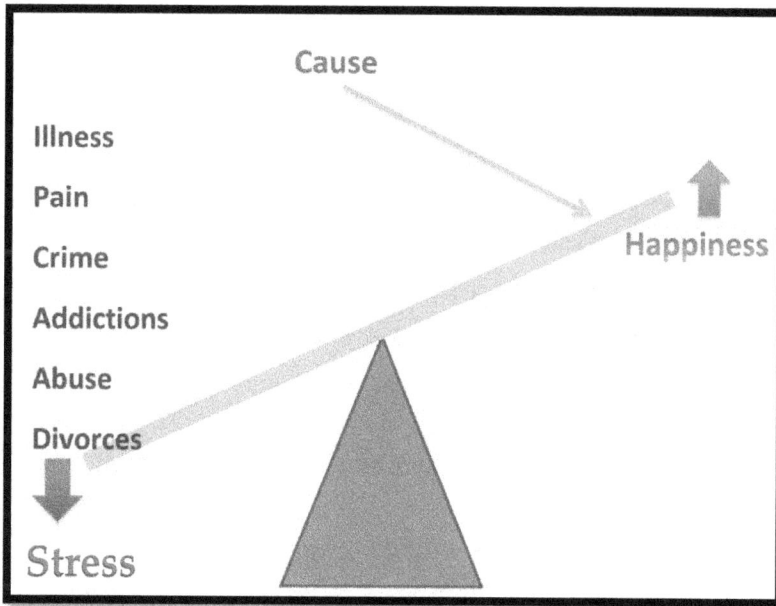

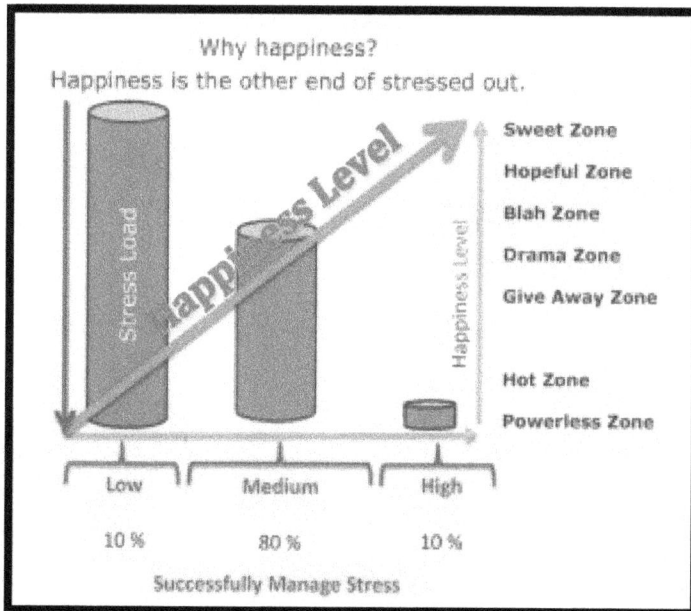

See the EGSc in the Appendix for more information on the Zones.

A Better World

My interest is in a better world for everyone going forward. We cannot impact or change the past but we can impact and change the future. It is clear that what has been done in the past has not worked well for many members of the human race.

We know that punishment (or the threat thereof) is not deterring crime.

We know that for most people punishment reduces emotional state.

We know that behavior declines when emotional state declines.

We know that almost all crime can be linked to low emotional states.

We know that behavior improves when someone's emotional state improves.

We know each individual has guidance calling him or her to better feeling states.

We know that this guidance is often misinterpreted.

We know that correct interpretations of guidance increases emotional state.

We know that there are skills individuals can learn that increase self-esteem, resilience, emotional intelligence, optimism, and internal locus of control.

We know that at risk children taught skills to increase resilience beat the odds and have better futures than expected.

We know positivity/optimism improves relationships of all types.

We know positivity/optimism is correlated to significant reduction in disease and chronic illnesses.

We know positivity/optimism increases the level of success one achieves.

We know optimism improves immune function.

We know optimism improves digestive function.

We know optimism improves cognitive function.

We know that many of the behaviors that lead to crime arise because of uncomfortable emotional states. These include, but are not limited to:

- Alcoholism
- Drug Abuse
- Smoking
- Murder
- Rape
- Robbery
- White collar crimes
- Abuse of spouse and children
- High school drop outs

I submit that the only logical, ethical, educated decision is to change the way we address undesired behaviors. The moral thing to do is to teach children (and as many adults as possible) to manage their own emotional states to comfortable levels with the confidence that even when the present situation feels awful, that they have the skill necessary to return to a comfortable emotional state without resorting to socially undesired behaviors.

The right response to undesired behaviors is intervention with the intent of helping the individual return to a better emotional state. This should begin with children at a young age and be reinforced by parents, teachers and the various systems that interact with individuals who exhibit behaviors that society does not support.

Additionally, all rehabilitation programs (whether from substance abuse or incarceration) should include training that empowers individuals to manage their emotional state without resorting to socially undesired behaviors.

Community leaders and schools should lead the charge. Religious institutions could take the lead if they are willing to look at the teachings of their own faith in a way that allows them to see that their faith speaks of guidance and that perhaps leaders in the distant past chose to diminish the focus on that aspect of their worldview. Although a concerted effort will bring about the greatest beneficial changes in the shortest period of time, nothing stands in the way of any individual, even one who is currently incarcerated, from being able to begin more accurately interpreting his or her emotions, understanding the guidance being received and developing skills that enable increasingly positive emotional states to be achieved and sustained.

If we do not do this, we are failing in our charge to do what we can to make the world a better place for those who come after us. Eventually the tipping point will come and this change will occur. The only question that remains is whether we are brave enough and bold enough to be the pioneers.

Understanding how our emotions impact our behavior and focusing on helping one another reach and sustain ourselves at higher emotional levels will have a tremendous positive impact on the future.

Success requires that we set our intentions on the loftier goal of creating a better world and cling less to the *need* to have been right in our opinions and judgments in the past.

Celebrate knowing new knowledge rather than regretting what we did not know in the past. Everyone has always done the best he or she could in the moment. Even during times when *the best in the moment* is not good, it was the best possibility for them at that moment. Their best in other moments could be better. Emotional state greatly impacts *the best in the moment* for each of us, which is one reason that maintaining a high emotional state should be an individual priority.

There is never a time in life when we know everything. Like children who gain new knowledge as they learn to walk, we are continuously gaining new knowledge as we live and are exposed to new concepts, ideas, experiences, and scientific discoveries. Embrace the new knowledge and leave any regrets for what you once did not know in the past. If you know enough to regret something now, the person you are also knows more than that person you used to be knew. Love who you are and whom you are becoming.

A Note about Religious Beliefs

On the surface, it will appear that the conclusions of this book, that individuals are not and cannot be *evil* contradicts many of our world's religions. However, if a willingness to dig deeper and gain a greater understanding is retained, I believe the concepts outlined herein lead to a greater understanding of the existing religious texts of many of the leading world religions.

The greatest conflict is between the concepts of *good* and *evil*—concepts I reject insofar as they categorize some individuals as *good* and others as *evil*. I see our behaviors along a continuum where *evil* behavior stems from sustained low emotional states combined with moral beliefs that make the *evil* behavior the path of least resistance. This is a significant difference from the traditional view that some people are just born *evil* (or seduced by the Devil to become *evil*).

As we look into the world, it is clear that not all individuals interpret religious texts in the same way. In many religious traditions, there have been divisions into separate sects as the result of differing interpretations. In *Perspectives on Coping and Resilience*, I wrote in detail about the specific text of six major religions as it relates to emotions as guidance. From my perspective, interpreting the texts as a reference to our Emotional Guidance makes more sense than interpretations that are more prevalent at this time.

I believe a deeper dive into the root of my thesis increases faith in the faithful, without requiring widespread fundamental changes to established beliefs. At the same time, it provides a stable foundation that allows peaceful co-existence of existing worldviews.

While a deeper understanding facilitates stronger faith among the faithful, Atheists are not precluded from benefiting from Emotional Guidance. Science, specifically quantum physics, provides a scientific basis for understanding Emotional Guidance that does not rely upon a religious or spiritual worldview. From my perspective, the way this solution perfectly aligns with differing worldviews is another sign that it is a valid conclusion.

Many widely accepted solutions are rife with exceptions. This solution exhibits the opposite characteristics. The more areas I have explored, the more it seems to be the missing puzzle piece—fitting perfectly into all areas of well-being and answering questions left by other, less complete, solutions.

Summary and Conclusions

What do I mean by "Is Punishment Ethical?" Although the ethics that we demand from the medical profession, "First, do no harm" is not traditionally applied to the legal profession, I think it should be. That is, I do not see how a system that seeks to punish individuals for doing harm can find itself above the law of not doing harm. It seems to me that the current stance is one based on expediency, politics, and possibly superstition since it has its roots in a superstitious era and the basis of the current stance has not been challenged. It is a hodge-podge of reactionary decisions thrust upon society

Although laws have changed significantly since the Middle Ages, we no longer draw and quarter people nor do we do many of the other horrendous things once done in the name of maintaining order. But the basic premise of the system, that punishment deters crime, has not been scientifically studied. It is clear from data on emotional state and behavior that emotional state has a significant direct impact on behavior.

The law has come a long way. There are many things that were punished in the past that are no longer considered criminal. There are many things that were harshly punished in the past that are no longer considered as egregious. However, despite the progress, I believe it is time to take a giant step forward. It is clear that punishment is not deterring crime. It is clear that many people (victims, the wrong doers, and the families of both) are harmed by the current system. It is clear that those who do wrong are, in the vast majority of situations, doing the best they can with the skills, knowledge, and circumstances in which they find themselves.

If we give individuals more skills so that they do not find themselves in desperate emotional states, their behavior will be better. It is a far more effective method of crime deterrent than punishment and has other considerable benefits. Unless and until we teach children skills we know will help even those whose trajectories are not good, society is morally and ethically responsible for the harm done that it could have avoided by taking actions they know would prevent many of the undesired outcomes.

Yes, for a little while longer, we probably need to continue with the current system but it would be wise to introduce skills that build resilience and positive emotion to those who are at low states as soon as they are identified. There are a lot of people who lack these skills who are doing things that make them a danger to others and separating them while they learn how to manage themselves into a better emotional state still makes sense.

But future generations, including those that are children right now, can have a better world. They can be taught about their guidance and far fewer of them will behave in socially undesirable ways. If we do not act now, the crimes of the future are on society for failing to give individuals tools we know they need to become more of their potential.

Imagine for a moment that politicians, in an attempt to balance the budget decided to cease public education—that they lost sight of the value, nay the necessity, of an educated populace. How would you feel about such a move? Would you imagine that the generation deprived of an education would be able to achieve to their potential? Would you imagine that the generation thus deprived might become unruly and difficult to manage, that they might resort to socially undesirable behaviors?

I submit that not training children in skills that are proven to improve the trajectory of their lives is no different than failing to educate them. What if we taught math but not reading in schools? Training children to understand and master their Emotional Guidance is that critical to a life well-lived, especially for those who face hardships and struggles to rise above early circumstances.

Training individuals about their Emotional Guidance would not cost what it costs for the things it has the potential to prevent for even one year. There would be an immediate shift, beginning with fewer new problems and a lessening of the initial states of illnesses such as depression. This benefit would build upon itself year after year, with each year providing a greater return than the one before as a larger percentage of the population used their Emotional Guidance effectively.

Increased positivity also has preventative effects on cancers, Alzheimer's, cold, flu, and other illnesses.[148] Increased positivity increases cognitive abilities[149] and the benefits to individuals and humanity of that are immeasurable. Imagine that someone has a mind that could cure cancer, but the person is chronically depressed because of a focus on the negative aspects of life. In that state of mind the cure will not be discovered. Give that person the skills to achieve and maintain a higher degree of positivity and the cognitive abilities that were mere potential while depressed can be realized. Imagine.

I mean it. Pause and spend a few minutes imaging how much potential is being wasted today because all children are not being taught skills we know would help them achieve more of their potential.

Based on what we now know scientifically, punishment as a form of crime prevention is not ethical because it does not decrease crime and creates environments known to increase crime.

There are so many resources that have helped me explore and understand both the benefits of, and the path to, a positive perspective. If you are interested in further reading on this topic, please see the Bibliography and my other books. All of my *The Smart Way* books add on to Emotional Guidance with processes that help individuals change ingrained habits of thought.

While many readers may assume the task outlined in this book is an insurmountable one, I disagree. I believe that if those who see it this way understood, as I do, that nature is on our side, that a self-actualized individual is our natural state[150] and that those who live lives that lead to crimes against their brothers and sisters are being continually called to the life we would prefer they lead by their inner guidance, they would see the potential of these recommendations and do all in their power to see they are implemented on the widest possible scale.

Most of the world sees punishment as the just reward for undesired actions—whether it is the 3-year old who spills her milk in an attempt to gain attention from a harried parent or the adult that commits a criminal act. The root cause of both behaviors is a desire to feel better from someone who does not know (or who cannot perceive) a better way to accomplish that goal, at that moment. With the understanding that bad-feeling emotions increase undesired behaviors the whole structure of punishment begins to break down.

We can rise above judging others' actions from our own perspective—from the knowing that we would never behave as they did—resulting in the erroneous conclusion that they are bad and we are good. It is not about good and bad. It is not about good and evil. It is about the impact of one's emotional state on behavior.

I am not suggesting that everyone who has already committed a crime should be set free. Nor am I suggesting that everyone who has lived a life that resulted in thoughts, beliefs, expectations, emotions and actions that are deemed criminal can be helped to a point where they should rejoin society and that they would be benign or positive presences therein.

I am emphatically stating that a path to prevent so many from going down those paths in the future is now clear. The knowledge, skills, and benefits are known. I do believe the work is worthwhile.

For example, this year has seen a significant increase in mass murder gun violence and the media focuses on guns, but mentally healthy people do not accumulate guns with the intent of causing harm to others. Mental illness seldom leads to violence. After all more than 10% of the population is depressed in any given year and most of them do not commit violent acts against others. But, those who commit those acts are not mentally healthy. In the vast majority of cases, I believe that if the person had been taught how to understand his guidance as a young child, he would not have manifested the mental illness that led to the massacres.

By focusing on guns as the root of the problem, mental illness is ignored. Henry David Thoreau said:

There are a thousand hacking at the branches of evil to one who is striking at the root.

The root of mental illness is chronically low emotional states. Widespread understanding of how to accurately interpret Emotional Guidance will go a long way to decreasing the number of people who suffer from mental illness. Even hate crimes have their roots in mental illness.

I am also saying that the longer we wait the more lives will be destroyed—both those who will become criminals and those who will become victims. Will future generations look back and feel appreciation for our willingness to move forward with changing the social structure to incorporate this knowledge or will they shake their heads at our reticence and the heartaches and tragedies that could have been prevented?

So often, after a senseless tragedy hits the news people ask, why didn't someone notice? Why didn't someone do something?

We now have the knowledge and ability to do something.

The concepts in this book have far-reaching implications. When those implications are understood, the ability to improve human conditions around the world will increase substantially.

I believe there is more than enough evidence to support the introduction of Emotional Guidance to a school system with monitored results. At the same time, efforts should be made to teach as many parents as possible about Emotional Guidance. Positive results should be quickly apparent. Initial introduction into prison systems to monitor recidivism should also be implemented. If the results of these trials provide anywhere near the benefits outlined in this book, immediate efforts for global implementation should begin to the extent possible.

> Yes, how many times must a man look up
> Before he can really see the sky?
> Yes, how many ears must one man have
> Before he can hear people cry?
> Yes, how many deaths will it take till he knows
> That too many people have died?
> The answer my friend is blowin' in the wind
> The answer is blowin' in the wind.[151]

I believe the answer is now. Too many have suffered via a system that does not begin to perform the primary reason for its existence. If not now, when?

How to Help

First, practice using your own guidance. Using it will make you both an advocate and an example of the benefit of working harmoniously with your innate guidance.

If you agree that the time is now, please share this information and/or write a review on Amazon or Goodreads. Your reviews make it more likely others will read the book and understand how we can make the world better for everyone. This is a paradigm shift and it must come from a grassroots effort if we want to stop the unnecessary suffering now. If you feel inspired to do so, sharing information on social media will help build support for implementation.

You can also form study groups to help one another become skilled at understanding and using your emotional guidance.

Ms. Joy is an inspiring public speaker who would love to speak to your organization about how to implement this idea. She is also very open to working with researchers who are interested in validating the effectiveness of implementing programs to teach students, parents, and teachers about their emotional guidance.

Thank you

Appendix I - Emotional Guidance Scale (EGSc)
In general, emotional states can be defined (broadly) with the following feelings:
Emotional Guidance Scale (EGSc) [152]

Sweet Zone

- Joy
- Empowered
- Passion
- Happy
- Inspired
- Optimism
- Fulfilled

- Appreciation
- Love
- Enthusiasm
- Positive Expectation
- Trust
- Serene
- Secure
- Gratitude

- Freedom
- Awe
- Eagerness
- Belief
- Faith
- Satisfied
- At ease
- Upbeat

Hopeful Zone

- Hopeful

- Gratitude

- Upbeat

Blah Zone

- Contentment
- Apathy

- Boredom
- Dispirited

- Pessimism
- Empty

Drama Zone

- Frustration
- Overwhelmed

- Irritation
- Disappointment

- Impatience
- Indignant

Give Away Zone

- Doubt
- Guilt

- Worry
- Discouragement

- Blame
- Offended

Hot (Red) Zone

- Anger
- Outraged

- Revenge
- Provoked

- Rage
- Furious

Powerless Zone

- Hatred
- Insecurity
- Grief
- Powerless
- Hopeless
- Suicidal

- Bullied
- Fear
- Depression
- Learned Helplessness
- Melancholy
- Unimportant

- Jealousy
- Unworthiness
- Despair
- Guarded
- Unwanted
- Exploited

P.S.

Understanding how to accurately interpret one's emotional guidance is enough to change the trajectory of millions of lives. For the children who are taught about their guidance and encouraged to use it from a young age, it is all they need to achieve far more of their potential than they ever could without understanding of the meaning of their emotions.

Adults who have established habits of thought that do not serve them can use their guidance to improve the trajectory of their lives, but the process would be slower if that were the only tool they had available. I've spent the last seven years finding and developing practical methods to help adults shift more quickly. Those methods are described in any of my books that have *The Smart Way* in the title. For any adult who chooses to use only Emotional Guidance, it is important to understand that you have neurological pathways that make your current way of thinking easiest. I encourage my students to be very patient and expect that the old habits of thought will continue to be common on any subject where you have spent much time for up to 3 months. It could be less or more, depending on how ingrained the beliefs are and how diligent you are in using your guidance.

Be easy on yourself. You did not learn your current habits of thought in a day and you won't create new habits in a day.

Anytime you are feeling less than you want to feel, take your thoughts less specific (more general). You can also use a change of focus to change your mood, but changing focus, the easiest and fastest way to change mood, does little toward automating better thought patterns in the future. Finding new perspectives that feel better creates immediate and long term change.

I wish you the best in this adventure we call life. You deserve it.

Sources of More Information

I have several websites with information that will be helpful.

www.Happiness1st.com

www.HouseofPeaceandLove.org

www.JeanineJoy.US

www.AchieveAffinity.org

The focus of each website is on increasing Human Thriving.

- Happiness 1st Institute offers classes to individuals and companies that teach skills that increase resilience, happiness, employee engagement, lower stress, and provide other significant benefits.
- The House of Peace and Love for All is my ministry where I work on some of the projects that are closest to my heart, such as increasing peace in the world and increasing human thriving in a way that is open to members of all religious affiliations. I seek to increase faith not to convert.
- JeanineJoy.US is my author website where you can learn more about my books.
- Achieve Affinity is a non-profit organization I co-founded with my husband to bring the information provided by Happiness 1st Institute to schools and others who cannot afford the services of Happiness 1st Institute

I blog on all four sites and on LinkedIn.

You can follow me on Twitter: @JeanineJoyJoy

You can also follow me on Goodreads.com

Radio shows I've been on are archived on Happiness1st and I will soon be broadcasting a weekly radio show for The House of Peace and Love for All

Facebook: https://www.facebook.com/Happiness1st

Special Offer

I occasionally hold Introductory Sessions to introduce individuals, businesses, physicians and clergy to my approach to human thriving. Please come to one of the sessions as my guest. If the Introductory Session is not serving dinner, you may attend as my guest free of charge. If a meal is being served, I ask that you cover the cost of your meal.

If you would like to enroll in one of the *Premiere Programs* offered through Happiness 1st Institute, this page entitles you to half off the regular price. If you want to attend one of the pre or post marital pastoral counseling retreats, this page entitles you to 20% off the regular price for the retreat (not off lodging).

If you are or have been incarcerated and are willing to be part of a study, which will involve a commitment to answer questionnaires before and after participating in an online course, please enroll on my webpage. The course will be offered to you free of charge during the study period. Space is limited. You will be required to provide information to verify your history of incarceration, but no personal information that could identify you will be released as part of the study results. I am also seeking researchers who are willing to assist with this study.

Admit One
Introductory Session

Register at Happiness1st.com   Code: IPE2015

Definitions

There are a few terms it will be helpful to define.

Chronic Emotional State

Chronic Emotional State refers to the dominant emotional state of an individual. Emotional state varies but the Chronic Emotional State is the one the individual's beliefs (mindset) lead to most often.

Emotional Guidance (EG)

Emotional guidance is communication from Source letting you know whether your thoughts are closing the gap between whom you're currently being and your potential self or widening the gap.

Emotional Guidance System (EGS)

Your emotions are a guidance system designed to let you know whether you are on course toward self-realization, veering off course or heading away from your desired destination.

Emotional Guidance Scale (EGSc)

The EGSc is a compilation of scales used by a variety of teachers including David Hawkins, L. Ron Hubbard, and Abraham-Hicks. The zones are my addition. The science supporting the Emotional Guidance Scale, or that emotions provide guidance, did not exist when the earlier scales were created. I have applied the science explaining the scale to their earlier works and found the Abraham-Hicks scale most closely matches current science. All emotions could be placed on the scale. It is simplified to reflect emotions that are similar in degrees of empowerment in each zone. The higher a person is on the EGSc the better his mind, body, and spirit feel and function. The lower a person is on the EGSc the less effective his mind, body, and spirit feels and functions.

Emotional Set Point

Emotional set point is the chronic emotion you maintain on a specific topic. Your Emotional Set Point is not the same on every topic.

Emotional Stance or Emotional State (ES)

Emotional stance is the in-the-moment emotional state. It is the emotional response one feels to his or her thoughts about the subject. Changing the perspective from which one views the situation changes the Emotional State.

Mood
See Emotional Stance or Emotional State (ES)

Source (God):
Source is the name I most commonly refer to what many people call God. Take Source to mean whatever your definition of God is.

Vibration
Everything in the Universe is moving, or vibrating, at varying speeds (frequencies). Matching frequencies are attracted to one another. When you're at a high vibration your thoughts are more positive. When you're at a low vibration, your thoughts are darker and less empowered.

We have the ability to adjust our frequency by changing our thoughts. We can train our unconscious mind to focus in ways that are more positive and allow it to do the heavy lifting of maintaining good feeling vibrations for us.

Bibliography

Abraham-Hicks (Performer). (January 22, 2010 Quote from Abraham-Hicks - YouTube. (n.d.). Retrieved from http://www.youtube.com/watch?v=H2Xh_rVHr80). Chicago, January 22, 2010. [E. Hicks, & J. Hicks, Conductors] [CD]. Chicago, IL, USA. Retrieved from http://www.youtube.com/watch?v=H2Xh_rVHr80

Abraham-Hicks. (Many). *Core or Common Concept from The Teachings of Abraham books, CDs, and live events.* Various: Abraham-Hicks and/or Hay House.

Achor, S. (2010). *The Happiness Advantage: Seven Principles of Positive Psychology That Fuel Success and Performance at Work.* Random House.

Allen, J. (2007). *As A Man Thinketh.* Wilder Publications.

American Heart Association (AHA). (2009). *Making Progress: Making a Difference CDC Heart Disease and Stroke Prevention Program.* AHA. Retrieved from file:///C:/Users/Jeanine/Documents/Research/Cardiovascular/Facts-CDC%20Heart%20Disease%20and%20Stroke%20Prevention%20Program.pdf

American Psychiatric Association. (n.d.). *DSM 5.* Retrieved from http://www.dsm5.org/Pages/Default.aspx

American Psychological Association. (2015). *Teaching Tip Sheet: Self-Efficacy.* Retrieved from American Psychological Association: http://www.apa.org/pi/aids/resources/education/self-efficacy.aspx

Anderson, D. A. (1999, 10). The Aggregrate Burden of Crime. *Journal of Law and Economics, 42*(2), 611-642.

Assagioli, R. (1965). *Psychosynthesis: A Collection of Basic Writings.* New York: The Viking Press.

Association, A. P. (2013). *DSM V (Diagnostic and statistical manual of mental disorders)* (5th ed.). APA.

Barn, R., & Tan, J.-P. (2012). Foster youth and crime: Employing general strain theory to promote understanding. *Journal of Criminal Justice, 40*, 212-220.

Batmanghelidj, D. F. (2003). *Your Body's Many Cries for Water.* Global Health Solutions, Inc.

Baumeister, R. F., & Beck, A. (1999). *Evil: Inside Human Violence and Cruelty.* New York: Henry Holt and Company, LLC.

Bender, K. (2010). Why do some maltreated youth become juvenile offenders? A call for further investigation and adaptation of youth services. *Children and Youth Services Review 32, 32*, 466-473. doi:10.1016/j.childyouth.2009.10.022

Bennett, T., Holloway, K., & Farrington, D. (2008). The statistical association between drug misuse and crime: A meta-analysis. *Aggression and Violent Behavior, 13*, 107-118.

Bergen, H. A. (2004). Sexual abuse, antisocial behaviour and substance use: Gender differences in young community adolescents. *Australian and New Zealand Journal of Psychiatry, 38*, 34-41.

Boehm, J. K. (2012, July). The heart's content: The association between positive psychological well-being and cardiovascular health. *Psychological Bulletin, Epub April 2012*, 138(4):655-91 . doi:DOI: 10.1037/a0027448.

Brandt, M. J., & Reyna, C. (2011, September). The Chain of Being: A Hierarchy of Morality. *Perspectives on Psychological Science, 6*(5), 428-446. doi:doi: 10.1177/1745691611414587

Browne, S. (2001). *The Nature of Good and Evil.* Carlsbad, California: Hay House.

Cauffman, E. F. (1998). Posttraumatic stress disorder among female juvenile offenders. *Journal of the American Academy of Child & Adolescent Psychiatry, 37*, 1209-1216.

Center for Disease Control and Prevention (CDC). (2010 data). *Suicide Consequences.* Retrieved from http://www.cdc.gov/violenceprevention/suicide/consequences.html

Chapman, D. P. (2004). Epidemiology of adverse childhood experiences and depressive disorders in a large health maintenance organization population. *Journal of Affective Disorders, 82(2)*, 217-225.

Corso, P. S. (2008). Health-related quality of life among adults who experienced maltreatment during childhood. *American Journal of Public Health, 98 (6)*, 1094-1100.

Counsellor, D. (1955). *The Uratia Book.* Open Source.

Darley, J. M., & Batson, C. D. (1973). From Jerusalem to Jericho: A Study of Situational and Dispositional Variables in Helping Behavior. *JPSP, 27*, 100-108.

Davis, R. C., & Smith, B. (1994). Teaching Victims Crime Prevention Skills: Can Individuals Lower their Risk of Crime? *Criminal Justice Review, 56*.

Diener, E., & Biswas-Diener, R. (2008). *Happiness: Unlocking the Mysteries of Psychological Wealth.* Blackwell Publishing.

Dietze, P., Jenkinson, R., Aitken, C., Stoove, M., Jolley, D., Hickman, M., & Kerr, T. (2013). The Relationship between alcohol use and injecting drug use: Impacts on Health, crime, and wellbeing. *Drug and Alcohol Dependence, 128*, 111-115.

Dube, S. R. (2003). Childhood abuse, neglect and household dysfunctino and the risk of illicit drug use: The Adverse Childhood Experience Study. *Pediatrics, 111(3)*, 564-572.

Eddy, M. B. (1875). *Science and Health with Key to the Scriptures.* Washington.

Edwards, V. J. (2003). Adverse childhood experiences and health-related quality of life as an adult. (K. Kendall-Tackett, Ed.) *Victimization and Health.*

Estrada, C. I. (1997). Positive affect facilitates integration of information and decreases anchoring in reasoning among physicians. *Organizational Behavior and Human Decision Processes*, 72: 117-135.

Felitti, V. J. (1998). Relationship of childhood abuse and household dysfunction to many of the leading causes of death in adults: The adverse childhood experiences (ACE) study. *American Journal of Preventive Medicine, 14*, 245-258.

Figner, B., & Weber, E. U. (2011). Who Takes Risks and Why? Determinants of Risk Taking. *Current Directions in Psychological Science, 20*(4), 211-216. doi:doi: 10.1177/0963721411415790

Findley, K. A., & O'Brien, B. (n.d.). *Psychological perspectives: Cognition and Decision Making*. Wisconsin University Law School. Retrieved 5 6, 2014, from http://ssrn.com/abstract=2438869

Fredrickson, B. L. (2001). The role of positive emotions in positive psychology: The broaden-and-build theory. *American Psychologist*, 56: 218-26.

Fredrickson, B. L. (2005). Positive Emotions broaden the scope of attention and though-action repertoires. *Cognition and Emotion*, 19: 313-332.

Fredrickson, B. L. (2010). *Positivity*. Three Rivers Press.

Gaarder, E. &. (2002). Tenuous borders: Girls transferred to adult court. *Criminology, 40*, 481-517.

Gabbidon, S. I., & Boisvert, D. (2012). Public opinion on crime causation: An exploratory study of Philadelphia area residents. *Journal of Criminal Justice, 40*, 50-59.

Garland, E. L., Fredrickson, B., Kring, A. M., Johnson, D. P., Meyer, P. S., & Penn, D. L. (2010). Upward spirals of positive emotions counter downward spirals of negativity: Insights. *Clinical Psychology Review*, 849-864. doi:doi:10.1016/j.cpr.2010.03.002

Goldberg, B. (2002). *Bias: A CBS Insider Exposes How the Media Distort the News*. Washington DC: Regnery Publishing, Inc.

Greenberg, P. E., Fournier, A.-A., Sisitsky, T., Pike, C., & Kessler, R. C. (2015). The Economic Burden of Adults with Major Depressive Disorder in the United States (2005 and 2010). *The Journal of Clinical Psychiatry*, 155-162. Retrieved from http://www.psychiatrist.com/jcp/article/Pages/2015/v76n02/v76n0204.aspx

Gromet, D. M., & Darley, J. M. (2009, March). Retributive and restorative justice: Importance of crime severity and shared identity in people's justice responses. *Australian Journal of Psychology, 61*(1), 50*57.

Haidt, J. (1992). MORAL JUDGMENT, AFFECT, AND CULTURE, or Is It Wrong to Eat Your Dog? Retrieved from http://people.stern.nyu.edu/jhaidt/articles/haidt.1992.dissertation.pub001b.pdf

Haidt, J. (2006). *The Happiness Hypothesis: Finding Modern Truth in Ancient Wisdom. Why the Meaningful Life Is Closer Than You Think*. New York: Basic Books.

Hill, P. I., & Lapsley, D. K. (2009). The ups and downs of the moral eprsonality: Why it's not so black and white. *Journal of Research in Personality, 43*, 520-523.

Hubbard, D. J. (2002). A meta-analysis of the predictors of deliquency among girls. *Journal of Offender Rehabilitation, 34*, 1-13.

Ito, T., & Urland, G. R. (2003). Race and gender on the brain: Electro-cortical measures of attention to the race and gender of multiple categorizable individuals. *Journal of Personality and Social Psychology*, 616-26.

Joy, J. (2014). *True Prevention--Optimum Health: Remember Galileo Wellness at the Root Cause for the 21st Century.* Charlotte, NC, USA: Thrive More, Now.

Keller, M. C. (2005). A warm heart and a clear head: The contingent effects of mood and weather on cognition. *Psychological Science*, 16: 724-731.

Keltner, D. (2009). *Born to be Good.* New York: W. W. Norton & Company Limited.

Khansar, D. N., Murgo, A. J., & Faith, R. E. (1990). Effects of Stress on the Immune System. *Immunology Today, 11*, 170-176. doi:DOI: 10.1016/0167-5699(90)90069-L

Kiecolt-Glaser. (1999). Stress, Personal Relationships, and Immune Function: Health Implications. *Brain, Behavior, and Immunity 13*, 61-72. Retrieved 10 8, 2014

King, Jr., M. L. (Performer). (1964). Acceptance Speech, Martin Luther King Jr.'s Nobel Peace Prize. Oslo, Norway. Retrieved from http://www.nobelprize.org/nobel_prizes/peace/laureates/1964/king-acceptance.html

Kohlberg, L., & Hersh, R. H. (1977). Moral Development: A Review of the Theory. *Theory into Practice*, 53-59.

Lansford, J. E. (2002). A 12-year prospective study of the long-term effects of early child physical maltreatment on psychological, behavioral and academic problems in adolescence. *Archives of Pediatric Medicine, 156*, 824-830.

Law Enforcement Leaders to Redue Crime & Incarceration. (2015). *Law Enforcement Leaders.org.* Retrieved from Statement of Principles: http://lawenforcementleaders.org/wp-content/uploads/2015/10/Statement_of_Principles.pdf

Lerner, J. S., & Keltner, D. (2000). Beyond valence: Toward a model of emotion-speci® c. *Cognition and Emotion 14 (4)*, 473-493. Retrieved 10 8, 2014, from http://www.tandf.co.uk/journals/pp/02699931.html

Lyubomirsky, S., King, L., & Diener, E. (2005). The Benefits of Frequent Positive Affect: Does Happiness Lead to Success? *Psychological Bulletin, 131*(6), 803-855. doi:DOI: 10.1037/0033-2909.131.6.803

Maier, S. U., Makwana, A. B., & Hare, T. A. (2015, 8 5). Acute Stress Impairs Self-Control in Goal-Directed Choice by Altering Multiple Functional Connections within the Brain's Decision Circuits. *Neuron, 87*, 621-631.

Mansor, A., Kirmani, S., Tat, H. H., & Azzman, M. (2012). Harnessing Positivity at Workplace from Perception to Action. *Social and Behavioral Sciences, 40,* 557-564.

Maston, A. S. (2001). Ordinary magic: Resilience processes in development. *American Psychologist,* 56: 27-38.

Maxfield, M. G. (1996). The cycle of violence revisited 6 years later. *Archives of Pediatrics and Adolescent Medicine, 150,* 390-395.

McCarthy, B. a. (2011). Get Happy! Positive Emotion, Depression and Juvenile Crime. *American Sociological Association Annual Meeting.* Las Vegas.

McCarthy, B., & Casey, T. (2011). Get Happy! Positive Emotion, Depression and Juvenile Crime. *American Sociological Associaion Annual Meeting.* Las Vegas: UC Davis.

McClellan, D. S. (1997). Early victimization, drug use, and criminality: A comparison of male and female prisoners. *Criminal Justice and Behavior, 24,* 455-476.

McCraty, R., Atkinson, M., & Bradley, R. T. (2004). Electrophysiological Evidence of Intuition. Part 1: The Surprising Role of the Heart," 10(1) (2004), pp. 133 - 143. *Journal of Alternative and Complementary Medicine, 10(1),* 133*143.

Messman, T. L., & Long, P. J. (1996). Child Sexual Abuse and its Relationship to Revictimization in Adult Woman: A Review. *Clinical Psychology Review, 16(5),* 397-420.

Moffitt, T. E. (2001). Childhood predictors differentiate life-coursepersistent and adolescence-limited antisocial pathways among males and females. *Development and Psychopathology, 13,* 355-375.

Nancy S. Wu, L. C. (2010). Childhood trauma and health outcomes in adults with comorbid substance abuse mental health disorders. *Addictive Behaviors, 35,* 68-71.

Nietzel, M. T., & Himelein, M. J. (1987, Spring). Crime Prevention Through Social and Physical Environmental Change. *The Behavior Analyst, 10(1),* 69-74.

Ou, S.-R., & Reynolds, A. J. (2010). Childhood predictors of young adult male crime. *Children and Youth Services Review, 32,* 1097-1107. doi:doi:10.1016/j.childyouth.2010.02.009

PBS. (2015). Altruism & Happiness. *This Emotional Life,* 1-2.

Peil, K. T. (2014). Emotion: A Self-regulatory Sense.

Piaget, J. (1932). *The Moral Judgment of the Child.* Rouledge, Trench, Trubner & Co., Ltd.

Population Clock Census. (2015). Retrieved from Census.gov: http://www.census.gov/popclock/

Rebekah E. Gunns, L. J. (2002 Fall). Victim Selection and Kinematics: A Point-Light investigation of vulnerability to attack. *JOURNAL OF NONVERBAL BEHAVIOR 26(3),*.

Richard W. Voss, D. M. (1997, Summer). Beyond the Telescope of Gender-polemics: Need for a Wide Angle Lens in Pastoral Vision. *The Journal of Pastoral Care, 51(2).*

Rivera, B. &. (1990). Childhood victimization and violent offending. *Violence and Victims, 5,* 19-35.

Roberson, D., Davidoff, J., Davies, I. R., & Shapiro, L. R. (2004). The Development of Color Categories in Two Languages: A Longitudinal Study. *Journal of Experimental Psychology, 133*(4), 554-571. doi:http://dx.doi.org/10.1037/0096-3445.133.4.554

Roth, T. L., Lubin, F. D., Funk, A. J., & Sweatt, J. D. (2009). Lasting Epigenetic Influence of Early-Life Adversity on the BDNF Gene. *Society of Biophysical Psychiatry,* 65:760–769.

Rubin, A. (n.d.). Psychological Stress and Immune Function.

Russell, D. E. (1986). *The Secret Trauma: Incest in the Live of Girls and Women.* New York: Basic Books.

Schnall, S., Roper, J., & Fessler, D. M. (2010, February 3). Pay It Forward: Elevation Leads to Altruistic Behavior. *Psychological Science.*

Seligman, M. (2011). *Flourish: A Visionary New Understanding of Happiness and Well-Being.* New York: Free Press.

Seligman,, M. (2006). *Learned Optimism* (Originally published 1991 ed.). New York: Simon & Schuster.

Shahba, S. a. (2013). Comparative Study of Problem-solving and Emotional Intelligence on Decreasing of third Grade Girl Students' Aggression of the Rajaee Guidance School of Tehran. *Procedia--Social and Behavioral Sciences, 84,* 778-780. Retrieved 2014

Shalvi, S., Eldar, O., & Bereby-Meyer, Y. (2012). Honesty Requires time (and Lack of Justifications). *psychological Science, 23*(10), 1264-1270. doi:doi: 10.1177/0956797612443835

SHERRILL, B. C. (Composer). (n.d.). Blowin' In The Wind.

Sinetar, M. (1986). *Ordinary People as Monks and Mystics: Lifestyles for Self-discovery.* Mahwah: Paulist Press. Retrieved 2014

Sisyphus Sysyphus. (n.d.). Retrieved 2015, from mythweb.com : http://www.mythweb.com/encyc/entries/sisyphus.html

Skenazy, L. (2014, 5 19). Land of the free, home of the scared: An interview with Lenore Skenazy. (B. Frezza, Interviewer) Forbes.

Smith, C. &. (1995). The relationship between childhood maltreatment and adolescent involvement in delinquency. *Criminology, 33(4),* 451-481.

Springer, K. W., Sheridan, J., Kuo, D., & Carnes, M. (2003). The Long-term Health Outcomes of Childhood Abuse: An overview and a Call to Action. *J. Gen Intern Med,* 18(10: 864-870.

Steven R. Gold, B. B. (1999). RISK OF Sexual revictimization: A Theoretical Model. *Aggression and Violent Behavior, Vol. 4, No. 4,*, pp. 457–470.

Swanston, H. Y. (2003). Juvenile crime ,aggression and delinquency after sexual abuse: A longitudinal study. *British Journal of Criminology, 43*, 729-749.

Timmons, M. (2002). *Moral Theory: An Introduction.* lanham * Boulder * New York * Oxford: Rowman & Littlefield Publishers, Inc.

Urantia Foundation. (1955). *The Urantia Book.* Chicago: The Urantia Foundation.

Waugh, C. E. (2008). Adapting to life's slings and arrows: Individual differences in resilience when recovering from an unanticipated threat. *Journal of Research in Personality*, 42: 1031-46.

Wikipedia. (2015). *Wikipedia.* Retrieved from Spock: https://en.wikipedia.org/wiki/Spock

Winter, D. A. (2007). Construing the Construction Processes of Serial Killers and Other Violent Offenders: The Limits of Credulity. *Journal of Constructivist Psychology, 20*, 247-275. doi:DOI: 10.1080/10720530701347902

Wood, J. (2013, 7 14). *Study Finds Gang Members Suffer High Levels of Mental Illness.* Retrieved 7 14, 2013, from Psych Central: Wood, J. (2013). Study Finds Gang Members Suffer High Levels of Mental Illness. Psych Central. Retrieved on July 14, 2013, from

Wu, G., Feder, A., Cohen, H., Kim, J. J., Calderon, S., Chamey, D. S., & Mathe, A. A. (2013). Understanding Resilience. *Frontiers in Behavioral Neuroscience*, 10. doi:doi: 10.3389/fnbeh.2013.00010

Citations

[1] (Schnall, Roper, & Fessler, 2010)

[2] (Ito & Urland, 2003)

[3] (Fredrickson B. L., 2010)

[4] (McCarthy & Casey, 2011)

[5] (King, Jr., 1964)

[6] (Allen, 2007)

[7] (Seligman,, 2006)

[8] (Abraham-Hicks, Core or Common Concept from The Teachings of Abraham books, CDs, and live events, Many) Abraham-Hicks

[9] Private Conversation SC

[10] (Lerner & Keltner, 2000)

[11] (Richard W. Voss, 1997)

[12] (PBS, 2015)

[13] (Maier, Makwana, & Hare, 2015)

[14] The concept presented here was introduced to me by Abraham-Hicks and I have heard it countless times, but I also consider it knowledge I know to be true. My life has shown me the truth of the concept I first heard from Abraham. Research in many fields, including motivation theory and depression support this view.

[15] (Peil, 2014)

[16] (Peil, 2014)

[17] Conversations with Katherine Peil, copious seminars with Abraham-Hicks, and my own life experiences support these ideas.

[18] (Batmanghelidj, 2003)

[19] (Abraham-Hicks, Chicago, January 22, 2010, January 22, 2010 Quote from Abraham-Hicks - YouTube. (n.d.). Retrieved from http://www.youtube.com/watch?v=H2Xh_rVHr80)

[20] (Wikipedia, 2015)

[21] This is influenced by years of teaching from Abraham (mostly) and other teachers but it has become my own my own by living these truths.

[22] (Skenazy, 2014)

[23] (Goldberg, 2002)

[24] (Fredrickson B. L., 2001)

[25] (Shalvi, Eldar, & Bereby-Meyer, 2012)

[26] (Baumeister & Beck, 1999)

[27] (Haidt, The Happiness Hypothesis: Finding Modern Truth in Ancient Wisdom. Why the Meaningful Life Is Closer Than You Think, 2006)

[28] (Haidt, The Happiness Hypothesis: Finding Modern Truth in Ancient Wisdom. Why the Meaningful Life Is Closer Than You Think, 2006) pp. 74

[29] The EGSc is a compilation of scales used by a variety of teachers including David Hawkins, L. Ron Hubbard, and Abraham-Hicks. The zones are my addition. The science supporting the Emotional Guidance scale, or that emotions provide guidance, did not exist when the earlier scales were created. I have applied the science explaining the scale to their earlier works and found the Abraham-Hicks scale most closely matches current science. All emotions could be placed on the scale. It is simplified to reflect emotions that are similar in degrees of empowerment in each zone. The higher a person is on the EGSc the better his mind, body, and spirit feel and function. The lower a person is on the EGSc the less effective his mind, body, and spirit feels and functions.

[30] (Sisyphus Sysyphus)

[31] (Lyubomirsky, King, & Diener, 2005) Add citation about kindness and positivity

[32] (Darley & Batson, 1973)

[33] (McCarthy B. a., 2011)

[34] (Wu, et al., 2013)

[35] (Dietze, et al., 2013)

[36] (Bennett, Holloway, & Farrington, 2008)

[37] (Barn & Tan, 2012)

[38] (Haidt, The Happiness Hypothesis: Finding Modern Truth in Ancient Wisdom. Why the Meaningful Life Is Closer Than You Think, 2006) pp. 76

[39] (Browne, 2001) pp. 3

[40] (Peil, 2014)

[41] This sentence, parts of the following sentence and parts of the discussion in Ought Self, have been previously published by me on LinkedIn (Pulse) and my website, Happiness1st.com My ideas are frequently a blog before they are expanded into deeper explorations. Also, the day I met Ms. Peil, we both used the children's game described here to explain guidance during our presentations despite the fact that we had never previously met or seen one another's work. Therefore, I do not cite that as hers.

[42] (Timmons, 2002) pp. 39

[43] (Peil, 2014)

[44] (Peil, 2014)

[45] (Peil, 2014)

[46] Abraham-Hicks inspired example

[47] (Lyubomirsky, King, & Diener, 2005)

[48] (Peil, 2014)

[49] (Association, 2013) (American Psychiatric Association)

[50] Abraham's definition of belief from many sources

[51] (Peil, 2014)

[52] (Seligman, 2011)

[53] (Findley & O'Brien)

[54] (Ou & Reynolds, 2010)

[55] (Ou & Reynolds, 2010)

[56] (Brandt & Reyna, 2011)

[57] (Winter, 2007)

[58] (Fredrickson B. L., 2005)

[59] (Keller, 2005)

[60] (Khansar, Murgo, & Faith, 1990)

[61] (Swanston, 2003)

[62] (Hill & Lapsley, 2009)

[63] (Winter, 2007)

[64] (Association, 2013) (American Psychiatric Association)

[65] (Winter, 2007)

[66] (Winter, 2007)

[67] (Barn & Tan, 2012) pp. 212

[68] (Allen, 2007)

[69] (Figner & Weber, 2011) Association for Psychological Science (2011, July 27). Who takes risks?

[70] (McCraty, Atkinson, & Bradley, 2004)

[71] (Gromet & Darley, 2009)

[72] (Eddy, 1875)

[73] (Eddy, 1875) pp. 23

[74] (Eddy, 1875) pp. 30

[75] (Rebekah E. Gunns, 2002 Fall)

[76] (Davis & Smith, 1994)

[77] (Steven R. Gold, 1999)

[78] (Russell, 1986)

[79] (Messman & Long, 1996)

[80] (Wood, 2013)

[81] (Barn & Tan, 2012) pp. 213

[82] (Garland, et al., 2010)

[83] (Garland, et al., 2010), pp 860

[84] (Garland, et al., 2010)

[85] (Garland, et al., 2010) pp. 850

[86] (Peil, 2014)

[87] (Seligman, 2011)

[88] (Keltner, 2009)

[89] Not all cultures divide the definition of color the same way. By studying the perception of color among cultures with different definitions it has been shown that colors that are close but in different categories are perceived as further apart than colors that actually have greater differences but are in the same category.

[90] (Roberson, Davidoff, Davies, & Shapiro, 2004)

[91] (Bender, 2010)

[92] (Bergen, 2004)

[93] (Cauffman, 1998)

[94] (Gaarder, 2002)

95 (Hubbard, 2002)

96 (Lansford, 2002)

97 (Maxfield, 1996)

98 (McClellan, 1997)

99 (Moffitt, 2001)

100 (Rivera, 1990)

101 (Smith, 1995)

102 (Dube, 2003)

103 (Felitti, 1998)

104 (Nancy S. Wu, 2010)

105 (Chapman, 2004)

106 (Corso, 2008)

107 (Edwards, 2003)

108 (Springer, Sheridan, Kuo, & Carnes, 2003)

109 (Edwards, 2003)

110 (Shahba, 2013)

111 (American Psychological Association, 2015)

112 (Wu, et al., 2013)

113 (Wu, et al., 2013)

114 (Wu, et al., 2013) (Maston, 2001)

115 (Shahba, 2013)

116 (Assagioli, 1965)

117 (Assagioli, 1965)

118 (Nietzel & Himelein, 1987)

119 (Fredrickson B. L., 2001) pp. 218-226

120 (Diener & Biswas-Diener, 2008)

121 (Haidt, The Happiness Hypothesis: Finding Modern Truth in Ancient Wisdom. Why the Meaningful Life Is Closer Than You Think, 2006)

122 (Urantia Foundation, 1955) (Counsellor, 1955)

123 (Mansor, Kirmani, Tat, & Azzman, 2012) pp. 561

124 (Gabbidon & Boisvert, 2012)

125 (Boehm, 2012)

126 (Khansar, Murgo, & Faith, 1990)

127 (Roth, Lubin, Funk, & Sweatt, 2009)

128 (Rubin)

129 (Waugh, 2008)

130 (Achor, 2010)

131 (Kiecolt-Glaser, 1999)

132 (Boehm, 2012) pp. 655

133 (Boehm, 2012)

134 (American Heart Association (AHA), 2009)

135 (Center for Disease Control and Prevention (CDC), 2010 data)

136 (Greenberg, Fournier, Sisitsky, Pike, & Kessler, 2015)

[137] (Anderson, 1999)

[138] (Law Enforcement Leaders to Redue Crime & Incarceration, 2015)

[139] (Population Clock Census, 2015)

[140] (Assagioli, 1965)

[141] (Nietzel & Himelein, 1987)

[142] (Haidt, MORAL JUDGMENT, AFFECT, AND CULTURE, or Is It Wrong to Eat Your Dog?, 1992) (Haidt, The Happiness Hypothesis: Finding Modern Truth in Ancient Wisdom. Why the Meaningful Life Is Closer Than You Think, 2006) pp. 28

[143] (Piaget, 1932) pp. 111

[144] (Haidt, MORAL JUDGMENT, AFFECT, AND CULTURE, or Is It Wrong to Eat Your Dog?, 1992)

[145] (Haidt, MORAL JUDGMENT, AFFECT, AND CULTURE, or Is It Wrong to Eat Your Dog?, 1992)

[146] (Kohlberg & Hersh, 1977) pp. 55

[147] (Haidt, MORAL JUDGMENT, AFFECT, AND CULTURE, or Is It Wrong to Eat Your Dog?, 1992)

[148] (Joy, 2014)

[149] (Estrada, 1997)

[150] (Sinetar, 1986)

[150] (SHERRILL)

[151] (SHERRILL)

[152] The EGSc is a compilation of scales used by a variety of teachers including David Hawkins, L. Ron Hubbard, and Abraham-Hicks. The zones are my addition. The science supporting the Emotional Guidance Scale, or that emotions provide guidance, did not exist when the earlier scales were created. I have applied the science explaining the scale to their earlier works and found the Abraham-Hicks scale most closely matches current science. All emotions could be placed on the scale. It is simplified to reflect emotions that are similar in degrees of empowerment in each zone. The higher a person is on the EGSc the better his mind, body, and spirit feel and function. The lower a person is on the EGSc the less effective his mind, body, and spirit feels and functions.

www.ingramcontent.com/pod-product-compliance
Lightning Source LLC
Chambersburg PA
CBHW081658270326
41933CB00017B/3212